CW00920218

Published in Great Britain by
L.R. Price Publications Ltd, 2021
27 Old Gloucester Street,
London, WC1N 3AX
www.lrpricepublications.com

ISBN-13: 9781915330086

The Pioneers Told Me Before They Died

Royal Pioneer Corps
1939 – 1993

23 Pioneer Regiment RLC
1993 - 2014

Andrew Nichol

Written during the global crisis of CoViD-19.

Contents

Foreword

VALUES could be defined as those qualities or ideas about which people feel strongly, and they can affect a person's decision-making, behaviour and goals. Values may make a person feel that something – or even someone – is worthwhile. Values may also define what is worthy, what is beneficial and what may be harmful. Values are standards which guide a person's actions, judgements and attitudes. Society shares common values, such as trust, courage, honesty, respect and freedom. Values are personal, emotional, can change over time and can differ from person to person. Values give direction and consistency to an individual's behaviour, and can help people to know what to and not to make time for. Values build a foundation, from which a person can form a relationship with the world. Values help us to decide right from wrong, good from bad, and decide between moral or immoral action. Values are influenced by our surroundings: school, home and society; T.V., music and books can also influence an individual's values.

> *"It's not doing things right, but doing the right things."*
>
> Andrew Nichol.

In schools, students are taught about British values, because it helps them to understand qualities, and how those qualities develop a young person's character. According to Ofsted (Office of Standards in Education), "fundamental British values" are as follows:

- Democracy.
- The rule of law.
- Individual liberty.
- Mutual respect.
- Tolerance of those with different faiths and beliefs, and those without faith.

The British Army, Royal Air Force, Royal Navy and other public services, such as the police, also have values and standards which are somehow linked to British values – for example, rule of law could be linked to the Army value of discipline, and the standard of lawful, acceptable behaviour. The British value of mutual respect may be linked to the Army value of RESPECT.

> *"We are what we repeatedly do. Excellence is then not an act, but a habit."*
>
> Will Durrant, *The Story of Philosophy*.

As a result of the CoViD 19 pandemic, some schools have reviewed their values and added "SAFETY", "RESPECT" and "READINESS" to them:

SAFETY: To create a safe learning environment, students sanitize their hands regularly. They may also be in year-group bubbles, preventing cross-pollination between year cohorts. Students and staff may observe social distancing and follow a one-way system around the school; all students avoid physical contact with their peers. This is all to create a safe environment.

RESPECT: It speaks for itself, though a Sergeant Major once defined it as: *"Treat people in the same way you expect to be treated."*

Be polite; students are polite, kind and take turns. They greet each other and concentrate in lessons. They become honest and learn not to make excuses. The same Sergeant Major also said, "If you do anything wrong, don't hide it; come and tell me," because if he found out from a third party, there would be a world of hurt awaiting! Nearly every Sergeant Major I ever met trusted people, and he or she would be trusted; it works both ways. There are times when soldiers may get into trouble for some misdemeanour, but if they had told their Sergeant Major in advance, the consequences would be greatly reduced.

READINESS: Students arrive at lessons on time, with their equipment, having completed homework. They become primed and ready for the next lesson.

There used to be a phrase in the Army: *"A good soldier is always five minutes early. An even better soldier is always ten minutes early, dressed in the right kit to do the right job, in the right frame of mind."* Be on time, wearing the correct uniform, carrying the correct equipment and books in a rucksack. Go to the toilet in breaks, not lesson times, do homework on time and to a good standard.

If students aren't safe, respectful or ready, they may become purposefully unsafe, disrespectful, and may display "unready" behaviour.

As an individual becomes older, their values may change from material values to the non-material values I have mentioned. There are those who may value money, or maybe a brand-new car, making those people materialistic (physicalism), but as they become more mature their values may change, and may make that person more productive. In the song "Material Girl" – written by Peter Brown and Robert Rans, then recorded by Madonna and released in January 1985 – the lyrics identify with materialism, an idea that matter is of fundamental value. At one point the lyrics say: *"Cos the boy with the cold, hard cash is always Mister Right."* Money is of great value, but is it more important than trust, loyalty or indeed any British values?

Certainly not the Army's value of SELFLESSNESS.

Introduction and General Information

The Sergeant Major is a soldier who has been appointed. The appointment is usually appointed to a Warrant Officer Class 2 (WO2). Depending on the corps, regiment or role of a unit, the abbreviation of the position will differ: for example, an infantry Sergeant Major's appointment would be called CSM (Company Sergeant Major); the Intelligence Corps and Royal Military Police would also have a CSM; the Sergeant Major of a squadron would be called SSM (Squadron Sergeant Major), a term which can also be used by a Station Warrant Officer and a Ships Warrant Officer, who would usually hold the rank of Warrant Officer Class 1 (WO1); the Royal Artillery would have a BSM (Battery Sergeant Major). There is also another appointment held by a Warrant Officer Class 1 (WO1), and this would be the Sergeant Major of all Sergeant Majors; he or she would be the RSM (Regimental Sergeant Major).

Many soldiers misunderstand the appointment of Sergeant Majors. For some soldiers they are seen as being there just to shout, rant and rave, as total disciplinarians. But to others, the appointment is totally respected and looked up to, as a position to work toward. The Sergeant Major supports the welfare and morale of all soldiers, and to become a Sergeant Major a soldier should possess valued qualities, of which this book highlights only some. Above all though, the Sergeant Major must care. A Sergeant Major should not be feared, but respected. A Sergeant Major doesn't shout; they inspire soldiers to become motivated. Qualities are what a person is born with; skills are what a person learns – qualities and skills can complement each other.

"STAND BY YOUR BEDS!"

This terminology is used to warn living-in soldiers that an officer is about to commence a room inspection. The term would be shouted down an accommodation corridor by a JNCO (Junior Non-Commissioned Officer) or an SNCO (Senior Non-Commissioned Officer) and would prime other ranks to stand at ease, at the end of their beds. Lockers would normally be closed and locked – however, an inspecting NCO or officer could request the lockers be opened. Prior to the inspecting officer entering a room, a JNCO would bring the room to the position of attention.

DOG TAGS

While on operations, all soldiers are expected to wear "dog tags", which are a method of identifying a soldier who may have perished on the battlefield. Dog tags are often called "ID discs". Often, prior to deployment on operations, soldiers would report to an orderly room in the unit HQ and hand over their ID card, in exchange for their ID discs; soldiers would sign for their discs, then on return from operations, they would exchange the ID discs for their ID card – again, when collecting their ID discs or ID card they would have to sign for them. If a soldier lost his or her ID discs, they would face the same disciplinary action and fine as they would for losing their ID card.

Dog tags are circular discs (not rectangular) with the following information embossed into them:

- Blood group.
- Service number (6 digits for Officers; 8 digits for other ranks).

- Family name.
- Initials.
- Religion.

After a skirmish or a battle, the remains of soldiers would have their dog tags removed and details would be recorded; one dog tag would be placed on the soldier's boot and the other attached to the body-bag containing the soldier's remains, which would then be placed in an area shaped like a square, prior to temporary burial in a grave of the soldier's religion.

The tags also identify a soldier to other nations, if they should be captured by enemy forces, but there are no markings on the tags to indicate rank or trade to the enemy.

There is a process which any army must follow, with regards to prisoners of war, which is usually coordinated by respective Red Cross or Red Crescent societies, and one of the responsibilities of Sergeant Majors (on the battlefield) might be to arrange temporary burial and funerals for fallen soldiers. I know many RSMs who have had to arrange funerals for the fallen in their units. The qualities needed to organize a funeral for their soldiers require the Sergeant Major to be empathic, considerate, benevolent and compassionate.

To the public, a parade square may be just an assembly area, or even a car park, but for military personnel a parade square is actually a sacred and respected ground. Historically in the British Army, when the retreat was sounded after a battle, the unit would assemble to form a hollow square and do a roll call, to account for everyone. A works party would then be sent out to retrieve the perished or fallen comrades; the remains of the fallen were then placed within the perimeter of the square and guarded. At one end of the square, the Union flag would be hoisted, along with the colours of that unit or battalion. No one would use the area as a thoroughfare. Today, the parade ground represents this square, and is deemed hallowed ground. It honours the sacrifices of the fallen, and the area is respected by all military personnel.

This book is about lots of people who would have an influence on the life of an individual. Each chapter is based on facts and actual events, with a touch of elaboration here and there. This book may help the reader to pause and reflect on his or her own life, and to help people – not to be materialistic, but to value the awesome qualities they already have, and to identify the qualities that other people have.

It would be true to say that animal lovers can identify qualities in their pets, and I believe that when you look into the eyes of a pet dog, you may be staring into the very soul of loyalty, in its purest form. I did in Crackers and Sid (two springer spaniels) and possibly in several other animals; all have their own character, much as people do. Our pets may learn from us, but it is true to say that we – as pet mums and dads – also learn from them; loyalty and trust work both ways.

I am the sort of person who, at a young age, didn't really possess the quality of confidence, but being exposed to life in the forces my confidence developed. Everyone I became friends with had something about them which made them priceless, and their qualities would rub off on me and other people. A Padre once said to me that everyone, both servicemen/women and civilians alike, are unique, but sometimes people lose confidence in themselves, and believe that they are of no use. But generally this is because those individuals are already awesome – they just don't realize it.

I have borne witness to some awesome events and to some horrific events. In the forces, I was an instructor with no academic qualifications, and I wanted to de-thick myself. My Padre pushed me to attempt GCSEs, followed by an access course, with a view to going to university. The more I learnt, the more my confidence strengthened.

There are 14 chapters in this book, all with a title, and most featuring a quote, highlighting qualities valued by the forces. Some of this book may be funny, some of it may be sad, and there is terminology that some readers may not understand. I have been in the world of secondary education since 2004, and there are acronyms and abbreviations schools and examination boards use which I don't have a clue about – for this reason I have included a Glossary. This is an easy book to read, making it suitable for any reader.

Please enjoy, reflect and pass on the awesome qualities that you have.

Chapter 1

Early Days

Her Majesty Queen Elizabeth II once said:

"You have to learn to stand up for yourself and what you believe in, and sometimes – pardon my language – kick some arse!"

LOYALTY is one of the Army's values:

"Loyalty is about supporting a team, looking after and helping each other, even when the going gets tough. In return, the members of that team will do the same for you."

I am Mark. I started life being born near York; it was about 4:00 a.m. (or should I say 0400 hours) on 17th June 1964. Naturally I can't remember much about the event or what was happening, but I'm sure my mother would have been wide awake and in a lot of pain; nevertheless, out I popped. It was summer and, according to what might have been the Met Office weather report, it was going to be a nice day. Then *boom*, here I was, probably screaming or crying, like most newborn babies trying to make sense of the new world around them (scientists have discovered that newborn babies don't cry; they are actually singing).

My earliest memory might have been my great grandmother on my mum's side; she would become known to me as "Little Gran". I seem to remember looking up toward someone – a lady who appeared to be pushing me in what could have been a pram, from where we lived in Rawcliffe, on the outskirts of York, toward some old WW2 aircraft hangars down a lane. Green Lane was the road I was being pushed along, an old taxiway with potholes that you could have got lost in.

The house my mum and dad bought had been built in 1961 on an old airfield, only sixteen years after WW2, where they would have done repairs on Lancaster Bombers and other aircraft. The airfield had been opened on 4th July 1936, prior to the outbreak of WW2, and used a civilian airfield; then, in December 1939, the aerodrome (as it became known) was taken over by the RAF, and would be commissioned as RAF Clifton. During WW2, RAF Clifton was also a relief airfield for RAF Linton-on-Ouse, which is about 12 miles northwest of York. After the repair centre and workshops closed in 1946, the airfield returned to its former role (prior to WW2) as a flying club. But the Air Ministry charged high rent, so the club closed in the 1950s. The airfield gradually fell into disuse, then neglect and decay. York would never again have a functional airport.

Our house was in an ideal location (the yellow circle): my first school was Clifton Without (the red circle), and there was a fish and chip shop close to one of my schoolfriends' house (David), which was a two-minute walk away, a Post Office and two or three other shops, including a butcher's. At the back of our house was the old aerodrome; cattle would graze on its wide open, grassy areas. There were old pillar-box air defences, which my friends and I called "air raids", and there were old bunkers dotted around the old airfield. The main runway was still there, running north to south. There was also another narrower runway, running west to east, midway along the main runway, to form a cross. To get across, onto the airfield, we had to cross a muddy, smelly old beck and yes, much to my mum's disgust, I fell into that beck lots of times, while attempting and failing to jump across.

Overview of the airfield, believed to have been struck in a Luftwaffe raid (cliftonwithout-pc.org.uk).

On the other side of the beck was an old, redundant airfield hangar, which was used by confectioners Rowntree's as a storage facility, storing cocoa beans. Its doors were huge, hanging from big iron girders. Eventually, in 1977, the Yorkshire Aircraft Preservation Society took over the upkeep of the hangar.

I had grandparents from my mother's side who lived in Leeds, including Little Gran, who lived in a small cottage close to Leeds University. It was an old building in one of the college grounds, with a big, old wall, making it safe for me and my sister Louise to explore stuff.

I was lucky: I also had grandparents from my dad's side, who lived on a farm in the Yorkshire Moors. There were lots of hazards existing on the farm, most of which I was blind to, though I was particularly scared of the pit – an old quarry, only 300 metres up the road from the farm. My uncle Simon would tell me tales of a grizzly bear who lived there; he would say: "Ooh, you need to give the pit a wide berth; there's a grizzly in there." It was only half a mile or so to the nearest village, but I listened to the advice I was given, and kept well clear of the pit when walking to visit friends. I actually walked close to three miles there, using a wood line to keep me hidden from the pit, and three miles back. At the end of the day, after eating my tea, I slept like a log.

My Leeds grandparents were townies, but it was awesome travelling on the train from York to Leeds. I always had a good idea about where I was, geographically. While on the train from York we would pass Cross Gates, where there was an Ordnance factory, which I was fascinated by. They built our state-of-the-art, most advanced tank, the Chieftain. The tanks were often lined up, but with huge canvas covers hiding them, which was a bit disappointing. Having arrived in Leeds, we would catch a bus to The Dutton's Arms public house, then walk around to Granny and Grandad's.

Grandad was fascinating. He had been a Desert Rat in WW2… a soldier! He told me stories about some fella called Rommel, who was a German general and a good leader, respected equally by his own forces and our own. I didn't for one second think then that one day, in November 2016, I would invite one of Rommel's old soldiers to a school remembrance assembly.

Over the road from Granny and Grandad's was Becket's Park. It was huge. There was a footpath which went through the park, past some tennis courts and my mother's old school, then toward some college buildings. I could run around anywhere within the boundaries of the park; there were trees to climb, conkers to pick and even the odd apple tree to scrump apples from. My mum and her best friend had long ago made a treehouse in the grounds of the park, with the help of Grandad, and it was still there, even when I reached my teens.

Little Gran would eventually move from her wonderful home to Queenswood Court, a high-rise block of flats. She lived on the 9th floor, and when walking from her flat to Granny and Grandad's, I would be able to see her still waving, even as I reached my mum's old childhood home.

I remember attending a sort of play school; it was in someone's house in the Yorkshire Moors, where we had to learn how to write our names and how to count. I didn't mind doing the activities, but I only had a short tolerance to using a pencil to write. My first real school was near York, and I can remember my first day at Clifton Without Infants and Primary School. There were no buses to take kids to school, so we had to walk; I was now in the infants, and in September I would have been five years old.

To me, the farm was very important; there was always lots to do, all year round. I was too busy to go to school, and if I wasn't at school I would normally be at the farm. My mum and dad would have wanted me to develop in a safe environment, just like any parents would; parents want their kids to go to the best schools, make friends and eventually get good jobs and have children of their own… and, of course, to be successful. But, as a youngster, I thought I would never have kids – and in a way I didn't. I can remember my mum sitting me down, to explain to me the facts of life, but I wasn't the slightest bit interested in all that birds-and-bees stuff – I didn't want to know about reproduction at that stage of my life; I wanted to be outside on my bike, doing my paper round and going to Scouts. So, I never became a real parent – instead, I become a stepdad to Patrick and Jane, two amazing and very successful individuals.

Infant and junior school wasn't bad. I remember my very first teacher.

She knew everything! Mrs. Allot could play the piano, read stories and do sums; she even did our PE lessons! She reminded me of Little Gran, because she was the oldest teacher in that school. Mrs. Allot was probably my favourite teacher, and I loved her class.

David and Sigmund became my closest friends. At playtime, we would take it in turns to be the fruit or milk monitor; each kid was entitled to a small bottle of milk or one piece of fruit. I was beginning to interact with other kids.

Each year we would move up a class. I must have been in the infants for two years before moving up to the junior part of the school – which we might now call primary school. During the 1970s there were first-, second-, third- and fourth-year cohorts. Mrs. Robson was our next teacher.

Mr. Watson was the headmaster. He had been in the RAF during WW2, and I seem to remember him having a photo in his office, of him in his RAF uniform. He had been a Squadron Leader at the old aerodrome we lived next to. During school assembly, we would line up in total silence, then we would be taken into the hall, where Mr. Watson would play his favourite tunes on a portable record player; Ron Goodwin's Orchestra would be booming out "633 Squadron" or "The Dambusters", both units of the RAF Mr. Watson had an affiliation with. He would explain to us that, even though we were free from the potential Nazi threat which had existed just a couple of decades before I started school, we were now living in an equally uncertain future; our new enemies were terrorists, who were raising their ugly heads. Not to mention the Soviet Union and their respective allies.

Every day I would see contrails of aeroplanes at high altitudes, on their way to their North Atlantic patrols. These aircraft were Vulcan Bombers, my favourite planes. Each plane would have a payload of one bomb, which was referred to as "Blue Steel" – atomic bombs. The Vulcans would have taken off from R.A.F. Finningley, now Doncaster Robin Hood Airport. Each bomb had a hugely powerful yield.

The devices detonated over Hiroshima and Nagasaki (Japan) had yields of 18 to 20 kilotons respectively – the equivalent of 18,000 to 20,000 tonnes of the high explosive TNT exploding; they totally devastated the two Japanese cities and their surrounding areas. Our Vulcans now had devices well into the megaton range; a yield of one megaton is the equivalent of one million tons of TNT; nobody would want those going bang in their backyard! In addition to the thermal radiation, vaporizing everything at ground zero (the point on the ground directly above or below the point of detonation), there would also be the radioactive fallout. "Fallout" is the term used to describe particles of dust and debris which fall back down to the ground, from the mushroom cloud of a nuclear blast; if they fall on you, they can be brushed off without feeling any effect. However, exposure to the gamma and beta radiation is different and very harmful – furthermore, it can affect future generations of people.

Our secondary school, Canon Lee School, was next to the junior or primary school. I would have been eleven years old entering the first year. I never applied myself anywhere near as much as I should have done at school, but I did have one ambition: that was to join the Army. One of my schoolfriends, Simon, was the same age as me. He was one of those kids who liked martial arts, kung fu and all that sort of stuff, but the idea of going to Cubs, then continuing to Scouts, appealed to me more.

Cubs was each Wednesday evening, then Scouts each Thursday. That left Friday free to get home from school then travel to the farm. Whenever I went to Scouts I would take 5 pence, so I could get 2p's worth of sweets and have 3p left to buy some chips on the way back home. If you asked for scraps, you could get lucky and get a half or a quarter of a fish. Lots of vinegar, a touch of salt and I was set, with a big bag of chips; that was my supper. I wouldn't have been able to eat much else, because I would be stuffed.

Scouts taught me a lot. We learnt all about knots, putting up huge canvas tents and going on camps. You could get your hands mucky and not get told off for it. We learnt how to work as an efficient team; we looked after each other. Each year, during Easter, we had "bob a job" week, when we would knock on people's doors and offer to do odd jobs, such as sweeping garden paths and clearing snow. And, yes, I said snow; it did very often up in the Moors, even at Easter, and especially up on Blakey Ridge.

During the summer months, my dad would take my mum, sister and I on walks often, either on the Moors or up in the Dales. The walks would usually include a couple of steep hills, but once up there it was great. Having reached the end of the walk, which was never more than eight miles, my sister and I would get a well-deserved bag of crisps and a glass of lemonade.

When it came to music, I didn't really listen to anything, other than what was on the radio. There were some catchy tunes, and sometimes now I hear tracks that I thought were good. Mostly, though, when I listen to music I am reminded of events which took place, or those tracks remind me of a particular place. Those people reading this, who were born in the 60s or 70s, may remember "Delilah", recorded by Welsh singer Tom Jones in December 1967, and originally by P.J. Proby in late November 1967. I would have been five years old at the time, and the track reminds me of my mum's kitchen on a nice, sunny day. There were blue and yellow curtains behind the washing machine and sink, and next to the washer was the gas cooker, then the pantry, where there were always nice things to eat – especially after Mum had done her weekly baking of cakes and other nice stuff. There were other singers and groups playing, too, like The Beatles and Elvis Presley; my parents had a record player, on which they would play Neil Diamond, and Mum's favourites *Grease* and the Bee Gees. I know only too well that songwriters and pop bands were and still are incredibly successful, because their music is still being sold today, but aren't other musicians, like Beethoven and all the other great composers, still selling their music? Most of the music I listened to on the radio didn't really float my boat; it wasn't until I reached the 4th year (nowadays it would be year 10) that I started to listen to and develop an interest in music.

Sigmund – Ziggy – only lived in the next street to us, so I could easily and safely hop on my skateboard and visit him. We both had skateboards, but his street had a nice, smooth surface, with hardly any grit or stones which might trip us up, and it was much longer than our much smaller, dead-end street. I had made my own skateboard out of a plank of old floorboard, and one of my mum's old roller-skates nailed onto each end of the plank. Despite it being very basic, it worked, and other kids wanted to have a go on it.

Ziggy suggested saving up for stuff to make real skateboards. I had a paper round, so I could save some money from that and still have cash left to put toward skateboard stuff. On the way into York, along Bootham, there was a shop which sold skateboards and associated kit, and we would often look through the window, at the items that were for sale. The skateboards were very expensive, but if I saved I would be able to buy the wheels, and other bits and bobs.

The wheels I wanted were £30 for all four. They were all singing and all dancing, state of the art Kryptonic wheels, with S.K.F. sealed precision bearings; they were red. But I still needed something to bolt the wheels onto; I needed some trucks, which were £12 each. I needed to save £54 – that was and still is a lot of money.

But the weeks went by, and each week I found myself counting the cash that I had saved. I delivered the *Yorkshire Evening Press* to thirty homes every late afternoon after school, then at the weekends I delivered the *Yorkshire Post* to eight farms, which were miles apart on the Moors. My final paper was to Geoff, who would be sat at the bar of the Lion Inn on Blakey Ridge. Geoff was a shepherd, and I'd often given him a hand digging yews and lambs out of snowdrifts during the winter months. Having delivered his newspaper to him by hand, he always gave me a packet of crisps and a drink of lemonade, before I was on my way back home, to the safety of the farm. If I was lucky, the farmers that I delivered newspapers to would be along the dale-head of Farndale, and I could hand over the newspaper, then continue along the old, disused railway toward Blakey, handing out the newspapers on the way. During the winter it was often thigh-deep snow, but the news still had to get out, and the paperboy or girl would be a keyworker to make it happen. I suppose you could say that I had a very hard paper round.

I got eight pounds per week for my paper round after school, and twelve pounds for my harder paper round; twenty quid a week – not bad for back then. After a month, when Ziggy and I presented ourselves at the skateboard shop, I had sixty pounds in my pocket. It was the most amount of money I'd ever had in my hand; it was a fortune. Even now sixty quid is still a lot of cash.

"What you gonna attach your trucks to?" asked the bloke behind the counter.

"I have a plank of wood at home," was my reply.

The bloke told Ziggy and I to go and get our planks of wood. "I'm here 'til three this-after," he told us.

Within two hours we were back at the shop, armed with our planks of wood.

The bloke laughed and said: "Come on, let's get these bits of wood sorted out."

Ziggy's wasn't that bad – it was solid and he had varnished it in woodwork lessons – but mine was a sorry-looking old offcut of floorboard. I didn't know it, but the bloke knew we had been saving up, and he showed us a fantastic piece of wood, with a skateboard shape already sketched on it. The bloke had a son called Steve, about the same age as us, and it wasn't long before Steve was making friends with me and Ziggy.

"Pop into town," his dad said, "and I'll have a new skateboard deck made in about an hour."

So Steve, Ziggy and I walked the 200 metres to the Museum Gardens and into town. We started talking about music,

"What do you like to listen to?" asked Steve.

"KISS," said Ziggy.

I had no idea who they were, but Steve explained that he had some of their records. "Come on, I'll show you a music shop."

As we entered, I couldn't miss all the records on shelves and on stands; they were everywhere. I could hear music being played, and I found myself tapping my foot: it was Boston, who had just released a track called "More Than a Feeling". That record stayed in my head for a while, before Black Sabbath started up, with a track called "Paranoid"; Ziggy and Steve just smiled. If my dad knew I was listening to this music, my arse would've been grass and he would have been the lawnmower.

Before we returned to the skateboard shop, Steve said: "Here's a good album." The LP was called *Axe Attack*, a compilation album of various artists, like Judas Priest, Van Halen and Black Sabbath. And so I bought my very first record (as they were then known). Dad had a record player, but I would have to wait until he was out before playing it. Most boys of that age would've tried to dig out secret stashes of rude magazines their dad might have had hidden away, but I was more than happy listening to the new music I had discovered.

I can only imagine back in the old days – let's say the 1400s, for example – when mums and dads would have listened to music from that period. Musicians would have chanted, and the music would likely have had a religious theme, such as "Denum Verum", Latin for "Thee, God, we praise", a Georgian chant, which sounded like something you might hear from monks in a monastery. Then, decades later, Renaissance music takes over, and instruments such as a lute or a recorder, and early versions of a fiddle or organ may have been played. Then along comes Vivaldi with *The Four Seasons*, and the young people would have loved it, perhaps preferring to listen to a full orchestra. Can you imagine the look of horror on the faces of those parents? "Nope, yer not listening to that rubbish!"

I think the same might be true even now. As a new style of music comes onto the scene, kids gravitate toward it. The same would certainly have been true in my case, as I gravitated toward rock music. I may have bowed to peer pressure but I liked the sound; it made me feel alive, and well and truly awake.

When we returned to the skateboard shop, Brendan (Steve's dad) had made a lovely skateboard deck, and even fitted the trucks and wheels; I was all set. And, I only had to pay for the wheels and trucks; in fact, Brendan even knocked a bit off the total price, all because he knew how hard I had bothered my arse to work on my paper rounds and saved up. I learned a lesson in life that day: work hard and you will be rewarded.

Just before the Autumn half term of that year, my gran said: "Why don't you invite Ziggy and Steven here to the farm for a couple of days, at half term? There is plenty of room. And, play your cards right and you might be able to camp out for one night, in one of the sheep folds."

I couldn't wait to tell Ziggy and Steve about the sleepover. By that stage, we had been all over the place on our skateboards, and listened to all sorts of heavy rock music. Brendan said yes and so did Aunt Betty, Ziggy's mum. Steve asked if he needed to bring anything,

"Yes," I said, "bring your wellies."

As kids, we didn't call the parents of our friends by their first names; it was considered impolite and rude to do so. Instead, all my mates called my parents "Mum" and "Dad"; likewise, I called the parents of my friends "Mum" and "Dad". But Steve was new to this; his mum had been tragically killed when he was five years old, in a road traffic accident while on her bike.

"Do I call you Mrs. N?" said Steve to my mum.

"Nah, just call me 'Mum'. Everyone else does, don't they, Ziggy?"

"Yes, Mum," he replied.

My dad mentioned that it would be too cold to stay in the sheep fold for the night, but Steve, Ziggy and I protested and insisted that we would be okay. We made a compromise: instead of staying in the sheep fold, we kipped in an attic above an old cowhouse; it was toasty warm, there was a dim light, and if we needed anything in an emergency, we only had a short walk. Ziggy was quite a bit taller than me, and I wore an old pair of jeans he had grown out of, which were now mine; they fitted perfectly.

Two of my friends, Jonathan (Jono) and Mark from Farndale, joined us. It was a Friday night and we ate like lords, every one of us stuffed with fish and chips from Kirby Moorside, and loads of cherryade, provided by Jonathan's mum and dad (who were also called "Mum" and "Dad"). We had a battery-operated transistor radio, so we could listen to the *Friday Rock Show* on BBC Radio 1. Jonathan and Mark hadn't listened to much music, especially heavy rock, so I found myself quite versed and knowledgeable about the subject; that's when I realized that the music I was into was heavy rock.

We must have talked ourselves to sleep; I woke up to find the light still on, albeit dim.

There were five of us friends, in the attic of an old cowhouse in the middle of the Yorkshire Moors. Life couldn't get any better.

Chapter 2

The Joining Process

COURAGE is one of the Army's values.

> *"All soldiers may have to use lethal force to fight and even take the lives of others, but at the same time knowingly risking their own lives. It is also true that students at schools display courage prior to GCSE and A-level examinations."*

> *"It takes courage to grow up and become who you really are."*

E.E. Cummings.

> *"Courage is grace under pressure."*

Ernest Hemingway.

My sister and I were never allowed to watch the T.V. before going to school, but by the time I'd dragged myself out of my bed then eventually into the kitchen, the radio was on. Radio One would be playing a song called "My Sharona", the debut single by a band called The Knack; written by Berton Averre and Doug Fieger, it was released in 1979, from their album *Get the Knack*, and reached number one on the Billboard Hot 100 Singles Chart. Between tracks the news would come on.

I would never pay much attention to the news, but on this one occasion something engrossing was going on. I had never heard of the SAS before, but listening to the radio the news made me aware of events which were unfolding in London: the Iranian embassy siege, from 30th April to 5th May 1980.

I was walking to school when Simon caught me up.

"Have you heard the news, about the embassy in London?"

Simon then told me all about the SAS, and how they were the envy of other special forces throughout the world.

He then went on to say: "Have you been to the Army Careers Office yet?"

I said that I was going that Saturday morning; they opened each Saturday until midday.

As we got closer to school, Simon told me that he was going to truant school and go to the Army Careers Office now. I had already mentioned to my mum and dad that, at some stage soon, I was going to enquire about joining up. Now he said that I didn't have the guts, and dared me to join him. So, I decided to join Simon and skip school.

I was now a rebel! What was I going to tell my parents, when they found out?

Instead of turning the corner which took us along the road to school, we continued toward York. It was a nice day – cool, but nice – as I was trying to think of a story to tell my teachers. But, that was the least of my problems; how was I going to explain to my dad?

Town was about a two-mile walk, and once there it was easy enough to walk through York toward Micklegate. Then, as we got closer to the Careers Office, I spotted one of my mum's friends – and she had seen me! Shit, that was all I needed; my mum would know by teatime!

We continued our walk up Rougier Street, then right onto Micklegate.

Five minutes later Simon and I were both through the door of the Army Careers Office. No turning back now.

The recruitment process was reasonably straightforward: you went into the office, said that you were interested in joining the Army, went through the initial process and that was it! When we entered, Simon and I sat down in some comfy chairs, around three coffee tables which had lots of information about jobs and roles in the Army. I was hooked – not so much reading, but looking at the pictures. After about ten minutes, a Recruiting Sergeant approached.

"Can I help you boys?" he said.

Simon and I looked at each other, then looked back at him, and I said: "We have come to see about joining the Army."

The Sergeant then looked at Simon and said: "What about you? Are you here to hold his hand?"

Simon plucked up the courage and said: "I would like to join the Army, too."

The Sergeant replied: "But this is Woolworths, lads." Then he chuckled and said: "Come and sit by my desk; let's see what we can do."

The Sergeant took our details – name, age, date of birth and address – and he completed the form for Simon, reading the questions out, as Simon replied with his answers. Ten minutes later, when it was my turn, I asked if I could read the form and complete it myself.

The Sergeant said: "Yeah, okay, yeah." He handed me the pen and the application form.

I read each question, asking questions if I didn't understand abbreviations. Then, ten minutes later I was all done, and I handed my application form back to the Sergeant. Because we were fifteen years old, the form would be sent to our next of kin (Dad) for signing.

Having completed the form, we did a test which included maths, reading and writing skills, a dominoes test and a reasoning test: questions like, *"If Tom is taller than Susan, who is the shortest?"* The test took about forty minutes, and our sheets were taken away for marking while we waited in the reception area. Simon and I made sure our ties looked good and our school blazers were on properly, before we were called in, one at a time.

An officer introduced himself to us, as a Captain from the Prince of Wales Own Regiment of Yorkshire. He asked questions about my reasons for wanting to join the Army, and what job or trade I could apply myself to. My test results weren't bad; I had passed. The Captain explained my options, and that my application form would be sent through the post to my dad for parental consent. Once signed by Dad, it would be returned to the Careers Office, then I would be sent details about attending a medical at Imphal Barracks, in York.

Simon and I were given information leaflets about our suitable options, with instructions to read through, so that at our next appointment we had an idea about which regiment or corps to aim for. It was also explained to us that we would receive an appointment for a medical, then we would need to go to the selection centre near Harrogate. The Sergeant gave us both a "chitty", to prove to our parents and school that we had attended the Army Careers Office. I was saved; I didn't need to worry about excuses for skipping school.

It took about a week before my medical appointment letter arrived, along with my application form. It was addressed to my dad, all folded up inside a brown A5 envelope.

At teatime, the telly was always turned off, and we all sat at the table to eat our tea. Dad would usually open his mail after tea, sat in his chair by a window, which looked out onto the front garden.

"What's that letter, Dad?"

After reading it, he smiled and said: "Go and get me a pen, then you can take it to the post-box." Inside was a pre-paid envelope addressed to the Army Careers Office. He signed the application form and an accompanying letter, then got me to sign part of the form.

"Are you sure you want to do this?" Dad said.

I replied: "Of course I do, Dad."

He read through the information leaflets I had been given.

"Which regiment are you going to choose?" he asked.

"Dunno," I said.

"Well, you need to choose soon, because you're back at the information office soon. Just don't choose the infantry."

At school the next day, another friend called Paul (also known as Buggsy) told me that he had his selection centre date; it was only a few days away.

"When I get back I'll tell you what happened – then at least you'll have a good idea of what to expect when you get there."

Paul had chosen the RE (Royal Engineers), and Simon was always going to choose the RCT (Royal Corps of Transport). Paul asked me what I was going to choose – I still didn't know.

The selection centre was at Harrogate. We received train tickets through the post, along with a letter – or, more accurately, *"Joining Instructions"*. We would be there for two days and one night. While at the selection centre, we would attend presentations in a cinema, about all the regiments and roles within the Army. There would be a physical test, a swimming test and another written and maths test. On the morning of day two, we were to submit our options, then that afternoon there would be an interview before going home. If we were successful, we would receive a certificate of acceptance into the Army.

Simon caught up with me at break time. I was by the long-jump pit.

"My application form is all signed and back in the post. I have my medical on the third of May."

"Same day as my medical; mine is in the morning," said Simon. My medical was in the afternoon.

On the morning of the medical, I had a good wash and Mum had shown me how to iron my shirt. There was no dress code, so I went to the medical in my school uniform.

The doctor, who was in the RAMC (Royal Army Medical Corps), said that I was healthy.

Part of my medical included *"PULHHEEMS"*, which was an acronym for:

- *PUL:*

  measures an individual's PULSE.

  In the 1980s, your resting pulse rate would be taken, recorded and the measurement done over a period of one minute. You were then asked to perform step-ups for a period of five minutes, immediately after which your pulse was taken and recorded again, then again one minute later, and again after another minute, to measure the time it takes for your heart to recover.

- *HH:*

  a hearing test, comprising "hearing left" and "hearing right".

- *EE:*

  a sight or eye test, comprising "left eye" and "right eye".

- *M:*

  refers to mental stability.

- *S:*

  Refers to emotional stability.

The whole test was a way of grading physical and mental fitness, and may be conducted differently these days. For the *M* and *S* part of the test, the doctor talked to me, and assessed my attitude and answers to his questions. He asked if I'd ever had any head trauma, and what I got up to in my spare time; I explained in depth about the Scouts. I had an idea about the things I valued – trust; my friends; family – and explained that I feel some achievement when I have completed a task for someone else.

The doctor then explained that my results would be sent back to the Careers Office, and the next stage of my recruitment would be my selection.

Paul stuck to his word, and proudly showed me his Acceptance Certificate. He was going into the RE, though he would still have to do well in his exams at school, in order to go into the trade he wanted.

He said that the selection centre was good, and he had enjoyed it. When he got there he was shown to his room, which he shared with three other lads. They had lunch, then took a test to identify what trade they wanted. After that came a swimming test: tread water for a few minutes, swim around the pool twice, then get out of the water unaided. Then came the diving pool: they had to climb to the very top platform and jump off. Once they had done that, they would then go up again, piggyback somebody and jump. This was the part of the test I was most concerned about; how was I to practice for that? I then realized that I could go to the Barbican Baths and jump off of the top springboard – so, for the next few weeks, I did just that.

The Royal Mail used to deliver mail twice a day: early each morning then once each afternoon; on Saturdays, mail was only delivered once, and there was no mail at all on Sundays. On Monday 19th May I received a letter. It was the day after the Mount St. Helen's eruption (18th May 1980). The letter was from the Army Careers Office, requesting me to go to the Army Careers Office to pick up train tickets to Harrogate. I had never been on a long journey on my own before, though Harrogate was only a forty-minute train ride from York. I was able to get permission not to be at school on the morning that I had to pick up the tickets.

Within two weeks, I was at the selection centre.

We were shown to our accommodation; it was quite new and the rooms were gleaming. The NCO (Non-Commissioned Officer) who took us up there called out our names, and we would walk into our respective rooms. Having identified our beds (our names were already on the beds we were to sleep in), everybody then had to form up outside the main entrance to the block, dressed in whatever we had arrived in.

We were divided into two groups, and for the remainder of the day we had to do a round-robin of activities, like problem-solving, another test then lunch, followed by the pool swimming test; before our evening meal we had a strength test and a run to complete. Each one of us was then given a card which already had our name on it, to record our activities and physical test results. For the remainder of the morning, our group had to take another test, like the one I had done at the Careers Office. That test was then taken away for marking and compared against our initial Careers Office test.

Lunch was good; there was all sorts of food on offer. All the chefs were from the Army Catering Corps and their white uniforms were spotless; there were creases down their sleeves and they wore blue-and-white check trousers, with sharp creases ironed into them. After lunch, we had our problem-solving activity, while the other group went into the pool for their swimming test.

A Corporal was in charge of the problem-solving. Buggsy had mentioned to me that I should not be scared of stepping forward and saying, if I have a plan which might work. The problem-solving comprised five different parts:

1. THE GAP CROSS.

The aim was to get the team across a marked gap, using bits of rope, poles, planks and a box. The box, team and equipment all had to be taken across the gap.

2. CLIMBING A WALL.

The aim was to get everyone and a box over the wall. There were some lads that didn't quite get the idea of a team for that test; they showed off and got themselves over the wall, but didn't help the lads who maybe struggled. For the remainder of us it was a team effort.

3. THE BOMB TEST.

The aim was to get a bucket out of the middle of a big circle which you couldn't step into. That test utilized ropes, poles and loads of other useless kit.

4. THE SHEEP TEST.

All but one member of the team had to be blindfolded. These members were the "sheep"; the shepherd didn't wear a blindfold. The aim was to shepherd the sheep over several obstacles, without any verbal communication.

5. THE FINAL TEST.

Required half the team to be blindfolded, but able to use arms and legs, whilst the other half of the team had vision but could not move. For that test, the aim was to put up a small tarpaulin shelter.

All five tests were about being able to communicate and work as a team, with people you didn't know. The instructors made notes of who didn't help and who stood out, and they wrote their scores; they had indeed marked our cards. I had done plenty of problem-solving activities in the

Scouts, and there were two scenarios which I already knew the solution to.

After the problem-solving, another Corporal (who was a PTI) took us all to the gym and running track, where we performed strength tests and 1500 metres on the track: three and three-quarter laps. After a warm-up, the strength tests comprised press-ups, sit-ups and carrying items up and down the middle part of the running track. For the 1500-metre run, if you finished before the PTI you had passed – to be fair, he didn't catch us out by jogging too fast, and quite a few of us finished ahead of him. Any lads behind the PTI had to stay later on day two (the following afternoon), for a second attempt at the run.

Before we had our evening meal, we got changed into our trunks at the pool and handed over our cards. For the swimming test, we had to tread water for five minutes, after which our names were shouted, and we had to swim around the edge of the pool, twice. Having reached the deep end, we would then shout out our name before getting out of the pool; the PTI would be preparing our card while we got out of the pool. This was done at the deep end, using just our own strength and power, unaided and without using the steps.

Once the swimming test was over, we went into another part of the building, to the diving pool. This was the part of the selection process that I was dreading; Buggsy had been right about that top diving platform. A PTI demonstrated what we had to do, then it was our turn. There was a PTI at the bottom of the steps, who had our cards and recorded our names as we filed up the steps, one at a time. On reaching the top board, we walked to the edge, one at a time, then jumped; I was fourth in line. That pool was quite big, but from up there it looked small.

A PTI at the top said: "Go on, son; you can and will do this."

I plucked up the courage and went for it. It was at that point that I discovered something about myself: I was able to do something which took courage. Then, like a toddler who might say, "Again, again, again!" I actually wanted to do it again. The PTI had given me inspiration to motivate myself. Quite a few of the lads I arrived with that morning had gone home; some didn't complete the swimming test or even attempt the high board.

Buggsy had advised me to cover my balls with my hands before jumping, so it didn't hurt when I hit the water. He was right, because on my second jump I opted to piggyback someone, and when I hit the water it hurt – though only a little. I jumped off the next platform twice before we had to get changed for our evening meal.

Buggsy had given me some advice about attending meals: "Don't put too much food on your plate; the staff there will try to identify greedy people. The catering staff will invite you to go back up for more food if you are still hungry." I was totally stuffed anyway, but I did go back up and get another pudding.

That evening, after tea, we all had to go to a hall and watch several films about basic training. We also saw films about the various trades within the Army, as well as films about adventure training and the sports we could participate in – this included sports that I didn't even know existed. We were shown films about the tank units, and several officers talked to us all about their regiments, and the soldiers they had who had gone through their training and now got trades. I quite liked the look of the RCT and RE My dad had already told me: "Don't choose the infantry." I think he was biased because he had himself been in the RE. We had to make three choices. I made up my mind that I was going to choose the RE as my first choice, the RCT as my second choice, but I still didn't have a clue for my third.

The remainder of the evening was spent in our accommodation, being shown how to make our beds, then strip them and fold the sheets, before making our beds again. One lad had a problem with this, and couldn't understand why he had to do it; a note was made. We were also shown how to keep our rooms tidy – the NCOs said that this would come in handy for if we were to go through to basic training.

On day two, the instructors came upstairs and made sure we were out of our beds and dressed. I had already been for a shower, and there were other lads in the ablutions, taking advantage of an early chance to get ready before everyone else, though some were still in their "scratchers", as an NCO put it. As another lad called Pete and I were getting dressed, there was the odd snipe coming from the other scratcher, demanding that we be quiet; Pete and I continued to get dressed.

"Here you are, put some of this on," said Pete, handing me deodorant. "It'll meck ya smell good in yer interview."

He asked what my third choice was going to be, and I had to admit that I still had no idea. Pete mentioned the RTR (Royal Tank Regiment), and that it had been his first choice. "There are lots of other tank units, like the Cavalry," he went on to say. I thought that perhaps I could use the tank option as my third choice.

I was dressed in a smart pair of trousers, a shirt, and I even wore my school tie – now with some deodorant on I was all set, when a Corporal by the door shouted:

"Stand by your beds!"

That was the first military terminology that I ever learnt. It meant exactly what it stated: you stood next to your bed. Another instructor, a Sergeant, came in behind him to inspect. He was from the RPC (Royal Pioneer Corps). I hadn't a clue what they did.

The lad who had passed comment at Pete and I was now out of his bed, having a wash, while Pete and I were folding his sheets; they had to be folded, so that they could be exchanged for clean sheets, ready for the next selection course.

"What are you two lads doing?" asked the Sergeant.

"We're folding his sheets," I said.

The Sergeant smiled, made a note, then said: "Well done, boys. Grab your kit and make your way to the cookhouse for breakfast, then on to the training theatre. You will get some help with choosing your options if you haven't already chosen."

I'd never had a breakfast like this before. I was used to cereals, like Sugar Puffs, cornflakes or my favourite, porridge (though not like the Scots, with salt; I liked a bit of milk and sugar on mine). For me, breakfast was more of an embuggerance and a chore; I wanted to be out doing stuff, once I had bothered to get up. At home, I was used to getting up early – I had my morning paper round – though I did like a sleep-in until eight o'clock on the days I wasn't delivering papers. I decided I was going to have one of everything. Eggs were fried or scrambled, there were baked beans, two sausages each and two rashers of bacon. It was lush. I even had toast and some orange juice. There was also cereal, including Rice Krispies and… *ooh…*

"What's this stuff?" I asked.

"It's All Bran," replied the chef.

All Bran? I thought. *Isn't that what pregnant ladies eat? Not 'avin' that stuff!*

Once we were in the training theatre, our names were called out. We collected our cards and were instructed to go into one of two adjoining rooms. The room I had to go into, along with a few other lads, was where advice was given if you hadn't indicated all your options. There were two tables with sheets of paper on them, featuring our names and informing us of the time and location of our interviews. There were other tables here and there, with leaflets and posters of all the careers the Army had to offer.

An officer from the RAPC explained to us about pensions and pay, and a medical officer informed us about all the trades within the medical services. There were also an RE officer, a REME officer, then an RCT and an RPC officer from Bulford both came in together, all explaining their roles in the Army – I had no idea that I would eventually be in the same regiment that the latter two were a part of.

My interview was at half-past ten. I had decided that my final option was going to be the RPC. The film about the RPC started with them guarding important buildings, then there was a soldier on an "Eager Beaver", a forklift truck which could lift cargo over all sorts of terrain. Part of the film showed Pioneers in helicopters and on ships, so I thought it seemed like a good choice.

At ten o'clock we had a break. We lined up in the NAAFI, where we were able to buy the normal items you would expect to find in a mid-morning or NAAFI break; I can recall buying a can of pop and a clacky bar.

It was now twenty past ten and I made my way to the office, where my interview was going to be held. I was invited in and waited until I was asked to take a seat.

The officer was from the Royal Anglian Regiment. He asked why I wanted to join the Army, what I valued, then he asked me about the Duke of Edinburgh Award I had done whilst in the Scouts. He asked about the farm and if I liked camping, to which my reply was:

"Yes, I love camping, sir."

"Good," he said, "because where you're going you will do a lot of camping."

He mentioned that the RCT could happen for me, but not until the following Easter (1981). He then said: "You could go into the Royal Pioneers Corps," adding: "if you do choose the RPC, you will be travelling down to Taunton in September."

My reply was: "Please can I join the RPC, sir?"

With a smile on his face, the officer replied: "Yes, of course you can, son. Of course you can."

He signed my paperwork, I signed it, then he said: "Congratulations! The Careers Office will be in touch, you will attend an appointment to say the oath, then pick up your shilling."

Back in the training theatre, we were issued our certificates of acceptance into the British Army.

It was now Friday. After lunch, we were transported back to the train station and were on our way home. On the train, I couldn't stop looking at my certificate; I couldn't wait to show my mum and dad. I still had some exams to do at school... but I was in the Army!

The following Monday, I was on my way to school when Simon caught me up.

"How did you do? Did you get in? What was it like?"

Simon still had to go to the selection centre; he was there on Thursday and Friday of that week. I now found myself in a position to offer advice to him.

I said: "Don't tell them that you value your motorbike, and when you get to the diving pool, cover your balls with your hands." Over the next couple of days, Buggsy and I talked Simon through every stage of the selection centre procedure.

There was a mixed reaction from my other friends. Ziggy was going to continue with school to do his A-levels, but he was very brainy; Steve didn't appear to be interested in the forces, although that did eventually change, a year or so later. My other friends weren't at all interested; some of them had applied for apprenticeships, while others were going to work on farms – which is what I would have done. Other people still didn't know what they were going to do. They needed to make their minds up, because our last day at school was fast approaching.

When Simon returned from the selection centre, it was Friday evening, and the start of our final half-term. I wasn't going to the farm until Sunday afternoon. I took a couple of quid from my room and told my mum that I would be at Simon's.

"Don't be late back," she said

Dad gave me an extra few pounds and said: "Bring a load of fish and chips back."

"Thanks, Dad. I will be back by nine o'clock."

He turned and said: "Twenty-one hundred." I needed to start using twenty-four-hour time; it is what the military use, so I had better get used to it.

When I arrived, Simon wasn't in, but his older brother was. He was called Luke, and he had been in the Army for a few years; he was now on leave from Germany. Luke explained that Simon would only be half an hour, and I could wait.

Luke was in the RCT, stationed in Münster. I asked him lots of questions and he asked me what I was going in. I said I was going into the RPC.

"Oh," he said, "you might be joining my unit, 8 Regiment, in a year or two."

The house phone rang and Luke answered it. Simon was on the other end. When Luke's face lit up, I knew Simon had got in.

"So, that'll be two of you joining me in Germany, then?" He ruffled my hair and said: "You'll need to get that cut."

Simon arrived about ten minutes later, with a big smile.

"I hear you got in," I said.

Simon replied: "Yep, I got the RCT."

"Your brother said we both might end up in Germany with him," I said. "Where are you going for your basic training?"

"Same place as you: Junior Leaders, Taunton," he replied.

Luke offered to cut Simon's and my hair; he had some scissors and a comb. Simon went first. Luke looked like he was doing a good job, and even Simon was impressed. It took about ten minutes, then it was my turn. My hair was somewhat longer; it took about fifteen minutes. At one stage, Luke had to use one of his mum's baking bowls, which he placed over my head, saying: "Pull down on the bowl. That's it. Oh, it's looking good now; that should do it. There, sorted. How's that?"

I looked in the mirror, at the tufts of hair all over my head, some bits longer than others. I did look daft. Simon tried to fix my new haircut, but seemed to make it worse. The bowl came out again.

"As long as it's above your shoulders, you'll be fine," said Luke.

I looked in the mirror and said: "Mum's going to kill me!"

By this time, Simon's dad had arrived home. In his Scottish accent, he said: "What on Earth have you done to your hair, Simon?"

Then I appeared.

"Oh, my god! What have you done? Your mum and dad are going to go nuts. I think we had better ring, just to warn them."

Luke offered to drive me home and we got into his Mk.1 Ford Escort; Simon and I were in the back, Luke drove and their dad was in the passenger seat. When we pulled into our street, Simon's dad got out to get my parents. I could hear him say to them: "Come have a look at this."

Dad couldn't help but laugh and even Mum joined in, laughing their heads off, while Simon and I had to just suck it up and put up with it.

It was about 19:30 now, so I said I would go to the chippy.

"Not like that, you're not!" Dad said. "You'll scare the public."

Our dads offered to go while Simon, Luke and I had to endure my sister and mum laughing at us.

On reflection, it was a brilliant night. We all had fish and chips, then my dad got Simon's dad and Luke a tin of Double Diamond beer each.

He asked: "Shall we let these two have a tin each?"

Simon's dad agreed. We were still getting laughed at!

No prizes for guessing what I would be doing the following morning… Yep, I was going to the barber's, to have that mess on my head sorted out and tidied up. As I sat in the chair, I could still see my dad in the mirror, sat in the waiting area, his shoulders bobbing up and down as he was still laughing at me.

I vowed to one day get my revenge, and in fact I did later that day. My dad left me to my own entertainment, while he went to pick up some electrical equipment. We had driven into York, in a fully rally-prepared Ford Escort Lotus Mk.2. The engine was a Lotus twin-cam, with twin Webber 40 DCOE carburettors. It was a red beast, with cargo nets where the rear seats would normally be, to hold spare wheels in place. There was a roll cage and an intercom system, for the driver and navigator to communicate with each other over the sound of that engine. The car belonged to Keith, a family friend, who was an awesome mechanic for Sheddon Transport Ltd., whose name was written all over the rally car, as well as two big white patches on each door, so that numbers could be stencilled on.

Dad said he would pick me up at three o'clock from Clifford's Tower, which would save me catching the bus home. I arrived there at ten to three, and I could hear the car making its way to pick me up; bang on three o'clock, Dad turned onto the street to pick me up. It was quite an event for the public, seeing a highly-tuned rally car pull up. I got in, did up the full harness seatbelt and we were off; everyone must have looked around as Dad pulled away.

There was a set of traffic lights with filter lanes: one lane to turn left and two lanes to go straight on. These lights were notorious for staying red for what seemed like ages, and they changed to red just as we got there. As we came to a halt, a green Morris 1000 stopped next to us. The driver looked over at our rally car and nodded. He started to rev his engine, so Dad thought he would rev the car we were in. The gentleman in the Morris 1000 continued to rev his engine; his car was very powerful and had plenty of torque on demand – it needed it for the forests. The sound of the Morris 1000 was very tame, whereas the car we were in was loud and throaty.

"Brace yourself," said Dad.

They were going to race each other.

I held on as the lights changed.

The Morris 1000 pulled away, nice and casual, but we had stalled. My dad's face went crimson red with embarrassment – and now it was my turn to laugh. Dad almost begged me not to tell anyone.

Two or perhaps three weeks passed, and I finally got the letter requesting me to attend the Careers Office; I had to be there by 13:45 on Wednesday 16th July 1980. It was my birthday only a few days before that; I would be sixteen years old. I suppose they had to wait until I was sixteen, so that I could say the oath and sign for my fiver.

There were four other lads in the office when I arrived, there to do the same thing. One of them was a lad called Michael; he was also going to Taunton, but he was going into the infantry: Prince of Wales Own Regiment of Yorkshire (PWO). A Warrant Officer from the Royal Army Pay Corps greeted us and invited us into a classroom, where an officer explained what was going to happen.

We were each given a sheet, and we all rehearsed the Queen's Oath of Allegiance. When saying the Oath, you start by saying "I", then everyone remains quiet as each person states their full name, one at a time; once the last person has stated their name, everyone continues together to read aloud the remainder of the Oath. After our rehearsals, we each picked up a Bible, held it in our right hand and read aloud from our sheet.

"Congratulations, gentlemen, you are all now formally in the British Army. Please file next door and pick up your day's wages."

The room next door had a drum in the middle of the floor; our day's wages was the shilling. The WO wrote our names down on a sheet and we each signed next to our names; a Sergeant then placed a five-pound note on the drum, we picked it up then went home, with an envelope containing a travel warrant and *Joining Instructions*. The WO stated that we must exchange the travel warrant for a ticket at the train station, on our day of departure.

Before leaving the Careers Office, Michael said: "See you in a couple of weeks; I think we will be on the same train to Taunton.

SELFLESS COMMITMENT is reflected in the wording of the Oath of Allegiance, which is taken on attestation:

"I, _____ , swear by Almighty God that I will be faithful and bear true allegiance to Her Majesty Queen Elizabeth II, her heirs and successors, and that I will, in duty bound, honestly and faithfully defend Her Majesty, her heirs and successors in person, Crown and dignity against all enemies, and will observe and obey all orders of Her Majesty, her heirs and successors, and of the Generals and officers set over me."

The day of my departure to Taunton did come around fairly quickly, and on Friday 5th September 1980 I started my journey. The weather was good; it was a nice day, with just a bit of cloud and hardly any wind.

I got up to say goodbye to Dad, who was off to work. Before he went he said: "Don't forget to ring when you get to Norton Manor."

"Okay, Dad," I said. "See you in a few weeks."

And he was on his way. Mum was up shortly afterward.

I had a wash and brushed my teeth; all I had to pack now was my toothbrush. As Mum poured me some Coco Pops, the radio was on; a song called "One Day I'll Fly Away" by Randy Crawford was playing. The news came on; the world's longest road tunnel "The St. Gotthard Tunnel" was being opened in the Swiss Alps.

We didn't leave the house until 09:30 that morning. I had only one small case, which I had packed the day before. The journey I was about to embark on was the farthest I had ever been on my own; I was going from York to Taunton. I didn't even need to change trains. Mum came with me to the train station, and by the time we got there I still had forty minutes before my train arrived on platform 1.

I approached the ticket kiosk and handed over my travel warrant. It was a light-green A5 sheet which had *"MOD Form 1175"* at the top, details of where I was travelling to and even the time of the train's departure. I handed over the warrant, to exchange it for my ticket, and made my way with Mum to platform 1, with plenty of time to spare. I needed to get the Exeter train, which would stop at various stations along the route.

On the way to the platform, I recognized Michael from the Army Careers Office. His mum was with him, too, and we all walked together toward platform 1, both our mums continually reminding us to ring when we got there. As my mum introduced herself to Michael's mum, they both asked us if we had our sports kit, razors, a flannel, towels and other bits and bobs. My mum was somewhat worried about me joining the Army; there was always the possibility that I might get sent to Northern Ireland.

An announcement came over the tannoy: *"The train now arriving at platform one is the 10:25 to Exeter, calling at Rotherham, Sheffield,*

Chesterfield, Derby, Birmingham New Street, Bristol Temple Meads, Taunton and Exeter."

We were stood in roughly the middle part of the platform, and as each carriage filed past, I could see sheets of card on each door, telling passengers all the destinations. I didn't think the train was ever going to stop, but after what seemed like forever it eventually came to a standstill. I waited for passengers to exit, then looked at Mum; she had a look of bewilderment about her.

"You just be careful," she said.

"Don't worry, Mum," I said, "I'll be back in six weeks." I gave her a kiss on the cheek, then I got on the train with Michael.

The train didn't pull away for about five minutes, and both our mums waited on the platform, looking into the train. At least they weren't on their own; they would probably go into town for a cup of coffee.

Finally, a whistle blew and the train started to pull away from the platform. One last wave and we were on our way to Taunton.

Chapter 3

Basic Training, JSB Taunton

INTEGRITY is an Army value:

"Integrity is the quality of being honest, and having strong ethical and moral principles."

"Listen with curiosity. Speak with honesty. Act with integrity."

Roy T. Bennett.

It was 14:30 when we arrived in Taunton. It was only a small station, with two platforms.

There were soldiers there, immaculately dressed, guiding boys toward white coaches. A Corporal and a Sergeant were shouting out, "All recruits for Norton Manor, this way," as they pointed the way.

Michael and I got off the train and shuffled toward the coaches; a Corporal took our names as we got on. It was a very basic bus, and we sat on the old, green seats with our cases next to us, in the aisle. I could hear music being played from somewhere: "Woman in Love" by Barbra Streisand. It had only been released a few weeks earlier, in August, from her 1980 album *Guilty*. Every time I hear that track now I am reminded of my journey from home to Norton Manor Camp.

The bus ride took about thirty minutes. It was still a nice day, and I can remember passing a pub called The Cross Keys. I could see a range of hills, which I would soon learn were the Quantock Hills – oh, yes, I would soon learn all about the Quantocks!

Arriving at JSB (Junior Soldiers Battalion) Taunton, we lined up outside the coach, on the main parade square – I would soon learn all about that, too.

There was a Sergeant there from the Royal Pioneer Corps: Sergeant Hope. He said: "When I call out your name, go and stand over there." He pointed toward a footpath.

He reached the end of his first list and a Corporal led those lads away. He then continued with his next list. Eventually, it got to my name.

"Yes, sir!" I replied, and went to stand in that group.

Another Corporal took us from the parade square to our wooden billets, which would become our home for the next year. They were spider blocks, which had three rooms down two sides, with a toilet block in the middle. There were also two offices here and some storerooms. We were all taken to our respective rooms. The room I was in had eight beds down each side. There was a wardrobe or locker and a bedside cabinet by each bed – and it was gleaming. I could smell the polish which made the corridor floor very shiny.

The Corporal said: "Drop your bags off by a bed, then form up outside."

Outside, the Corporals showed us all how we would "fall in":

"So, gentlemen, when you hear the words 'fall in', this is how you will all form up. Look around and identify where you are within the squad."

There were three rows of us. Each row was referred to as a "rank", so three rows were three ranks.

Shortly afterward, another Corporal came out, then a Sergeant. "My name is Sergeant Wilcox," he told us. "I am in the King's Regiment and I will be your Platoon Sergeant."

I knew what the Yorkshire and Geordie accents were, but he was from Liverpool, and he spoke with an accent that I had never heard before.

Sergeant Wilcox continued in his Scouse accent: "You are all in 8 Platoon. These are my instructors Corporal Ferguson and Corporal Glennon."

Corporal Ferguson had a slight Geordie accent, while Corporal Glennon had a Sheffield accent. They were both in the Green Howards. There would have been another Corporal present, too, but he was on a course.

"Corporals Glennon and Ferguson are going to show you around the camp, and where to go if there is a fire." So far, our instructors were being very polite.

"Turn and face that way," said Corporal Glennon, "and follow Corporal Ferguson while we walk to the first destination. Try and keep in step with each other'; I will call out the pace."

We turned and followed, while Corporal Glennon called out: "Left, right, left, right, left, right, leeeft…"

Our first stop was the cookhouse:

"Hold it there, lads. This is where you will have your meals; this will be your entrance."

We then continued to the parade square:

"This is the parade square. We will spend a lot of time here on the square."

We eventually reached the three gymnasiums:

"You will also spend a lot of time here."

We were shown the cinema, the church, the regimental headquarters and the various company and squadron headquarters; we were in 8 Platoon, King's Company. We were shown the Armoury, obstacle course, Medical Centre and the NAAFI – there were four public telephone boxes outside the NAAFI. The instructors then took us to the Guardroom, where the "nick" – or jail – was. Then it was the barbers; my hair was short enough already, and was acceptable, but some of the lads had to get their hair cut, while the rest of us returned to our accommodation.

We were all asked to write a letter to our parents, to let them know we had arrived safely. Letter writing was compulsory, and had to be done each Sunday, after church parade. Our letters were handed over and vetted before they could be posted. We didn't have to pay for stamps; that was all done for us.

We were shown a noticeboard, just along the corridor, and each day there would be information we would need to read. Before evening meal, we had to look on the noticeboard to find out our regimental numbers: mine was 24576044; I was now Junior Soldier (J/Sld.) Nichol. We were all required to learn our regimental numbers and the address of the camp by the following morning. We also had to know who the following were:

- CO (Commanding Officer) Lt. Col. Mackintosh MBE.
- RSM (Regimental Sergeant Major) WO1 RSM Eastwood BEM.
- OC (Officer Commanding King's Company) Maj (Major) Albury PWO.
- WO2 Callister QLR, Company Sergeant Major of King's Company.

My first meal was tea. It was served on trays; there was a main meal then a choice of puddings, before we were free for the remainder of the evening, though we had to be in bed by 21:30; lights out by 22:00 (we all had to start using 24-hour time).

I went to the NAAFI to use the phone. There was a bit of a queue, and

I needed to get loads of 10p pieces. There was a jukebox there, and a lad had put on "Bat out of Hell" by Meatloaf. I started to make friends, and I even saw Michael; Simon wasn't due to arrive until the next day. I continued to recite my regimental number, over and over and over again; I had even written it on the letter to Mum and Dad. Eventually, it was my turn to use the public phone. I dialled the number and waited; there was no ringing tone. I tried again and still nothing. I tried a third and fourth time, but still nothing. Eventually, I hung up; I would have another go in half an hour or so.

I got myself a drink of pop, then watched telly. After half an hour I made another attempt at phoning home, but still nothing. I tried again, until it suddenly dawned on me that it wasn't my home phone number I was dialling; I was dialling my regimental number!

The following day was Saturday, and our first lesson was in the ablutions: we were shown how to wash, brush our teeth and shave; Sergeant Wilcox was in charge.

"This is how we wash ourselves in the Army." He filled up the basin with a mixture of cool and hot water. "Not too much water, and warm enough to put your hands in."

Having dried his face, he then said: "Right, you all have thirty seconds to go and have a wash. Go."

We all found a sink and had a wash.

Next, he demonstrated how to shave.

"Are there any questions?"

I put up my hand. Before I had even said anything, he said: "The answer to your question is yes, you do need to shave."

How did he know I was going to ask that question? I had never even needed a shave before.

"You all need to get rid of your bum-fluff," he explained.

Then he continued: "This is how we brush our teeth in the Army." We had one minute to polish our teeth.

After breakfast, we were all taken to be issued our tracksuits – they were navy blue, with *"JSB Taunton"* written on the back. We had to keep our sports kit, a smart pair of trousers, a tie and a smart shirt available; the rest of our kit, which we had worn the previous day, was packed away and placed in a storeroom – we wouldn't see them for six weeks.

That afternoon, we had to play football. The playing fields were about a mile away, in Norton Fitzwarren; we passed the Armoury and walked there, at a very quick pace. It is not a sport that I like, but over the next few weeks we were all required to take part in football, rugby, basketball, swimming and a court game of your choice – the idea was to identify which sports you might like.

That Saturday afternoon, we were shown how to use floor polish and bumpers. We were shown all the other block jobs, and told that we must read the noticeboard each day, for "Part One Orders" and "Company Orders", along with other notices.

The following day was church parade. We formed up outside our block, after block jobs and breakfast, then we marched to the church. We were greeted by a Major wearing barrack dress of smart uniform and a hessian tie. This was the Padre from the Army Chaplains Department.

The very first thing he did was put out his cigarette and say: "Right then, you lot, I'm an Army vicar and this building in front of you is a fucking church. When I say go, get your arses in there and sit them down. Stand by... GO." I had never heard a vicar swear.

Over the next year, the Padre would see us every Sunday; he would even come and visit us in the NAAFI. He was totally awesome, very funny and a gentleman. If we had problems, we could always approach him and he would help. In fact, every Padre I ever met was fantastic. Even when you're cold and wet through, or down in the dumps on exercises, a Padre will make you laugh. It was a Padre who would eventually become a good friend and put me on the path to becoming a teacher.

Over the next few days, we were issued most of our uniform: two combat suits, two sets of working dress, two pairs of boots, a face veil and a pair of putties, along with lots of other kit, a suitcase and a kit bag. Oh, and what would become known as a "crow cap" – this was our headdress: a camouflaged cap which looked a bit like a baseball cap. We were shown how to iron our kit, then, on the Wednesday morning of our first week, we put on our working dress for the first time.

Now there was no more Mr. Nice Guy from any of our instructors; we were in the Queen's uniform.

Over the next few weeks, we did loads of drill and were introduced to our personal weapon: the SLR (self-loading rifle). We could almost recite phraseology for our drill lessons. We had fieldcraft lessons and, by the fourth week, we were ready for our very first exercise in the Quantock Hills. It wasn't until week four that we were introduced to our other Platoon Corporal, Corporal Long from the Royal Pioneer Corps. He was from Dorset, only a few miles away, and spoke with a very strong Westcountry accent.

Part of our training included compulsory maths and English lessons, and toward the end of our training we could attempt part of the educational requirements needed to become a Sergeant. They were referred to as "Military Calculations" and "Military Communications", and if we were successful and passed them, we would have two subjects toward our EPC ("Education for Promotion") course. This was all done by the Army Education Corps.

After each day we were expected to attend hobby sessions. I had chosen German lessons, at the Education Centre. Over the weeks I became quite good at German. My tutor said: "If you continue to improve you could leave Taunton with a linguistic qualification. Colloquial German is a very good qualification to have." I made more friends from the various infantry units and RCT while doing my German, and by week four I had passed Basic German.

We only had two more weeks until half-term, when we could go home for a week. It had only been four weeks, but a lot of lads had already gone home, for one reason or another. The remainder of us were working hard, coasting along, doing as we were told and being the best we could be.

PT (physical training) was fantastic. I remember Corporal Savage from the King's Own Royal Border Regiment. He was an Army boxer – quite intimidating, but a brilliant Physical Training Instructor (PTI). He took us for our first APFA (Annual Personal Fitness Assessment), which was done in weeks one and six of training, then twice each term. We had the same terms as schools – autumn, spring and summer – and only one half-term, which was after our sixth week of training. After each PT lesson, Corporal Savage would say: "Fall in." He would then inspect us, ask us how we felt, then march us up and down for five minutes. He would always explain the reason for doing "beastings", as he called them, and this made lots of us want to do PT even more.

For my second hobby, I chose to do circuit training, each Wednesday and Friday. The instructors were still strict, but we saw a different side of them; they were friendly people, and they wanted us to get better. From time to time, there was friendly banter from all the instructors, both military and PT.

Week six was here, and that Friday we were going home on leave. But we had three objectives to meet first:

- Two APFA – week 1 and week 6, showing improvement on the second;
- Passing-Off Parade – a drill parade where we were presented with our berets;
- TOET – a weapons safety handling test, with the SLR and SMG.

I failed my first TOET on the SLR, as did half of the platoon, but most of us passed on our second attempt.

As for our fitness test, six of us nailed it. Corporal Savage explained the requirements and demonstrated each of the tests, which comprised (in no particular order):

- Sit-ups.
- Pull-ups.
- A jump test.
- Dips.
- Press-ups.
- Burpees.
- 4 laps of a 400-metre running track.

Corporal Savage told me off for showing off, then walked away smiling.

On the Friday we had our Passing-Off Parade. Sgt. Wilcox marched us up and down, then we were inspected by Sgt. Wilcox and Lt. Wild. In groups of three we had to demonstrate halting, left and right turn on the march, then one at a time we marched up to our Platoon Commander, halted, saluted and spieled off our number, rank and name. We took off our crow cap, replaced it with our beret, with its cap badge already in, saluted again, then marched back to our position within the squad. That Friday it was raining but, as Corporal Ferguson said: "Skin's waterproof."

After a successful parade, we were marched away and paraded outside the Company Office to get our pay. I had £35 to go home with; the remainder of our wages were saved for us, referred to as "credits". After our lunch, we got changed into our smart civvies and waited for our coaches to take us to Taunton train station.

I think the transport people in the H.Q. offices really did a good job of getting a whole battalion of boy soldiers – or "Brats" – back home on leave. We had two squadrons of RCT (34 Sqn. and 59 Sqn.) and three companies of infantry, and where you were from geographically in the UK would discern which company or squadron you would be allocated to:

- King's Coy were from the northern counties of the UK; northern regiments.
- Queen's Coy were from the Home Counties and south of the UK; southern regiments.
- Prince of Wales Coy were from the southwest of the UK and Wales; Welsh regiments.
- 59 Sqn. RCT were from the north of the UK.
- 34 Sqn. RCT were from south of the UK.

This would give transport planners – in terms of the rail network – a good idea about the timings of trains to Bristol, Birmingham, London and Plymouth, and whom to send on which bus. Our instructors even guided us about changing trains – wow, I had never done that before. It was likely that I would have to change trains at Birmingham New Street; I would need to check the card on the door of the train, when it arrived at Taunton.

I didn't have to rush; I just made my way to the platform that I needed. Even if I missed that train, I could be on another about an hour later.

Each time we went on leave from Taunton, it was the same procedure: I travelled from Taunton to York with Simon, and we both got on the number 9 bus from Rougier Street. My stop was first.

"Give us a ring tomorrow, Simon. See ya."

By the time I got home it was teatime; Dad was home from work and Vicky had been back from school for about an hour. She still had another two weeks at school before her half-term.

The next day, I found the self-discipline to go for a run. I ran down toward the River Ouse, then along for a mile or so, before picking up the footpath I used to use on school cross-country runs. I could never run all the way round that route when I was at school, but now I found it very easy; I ran close to eight miles.

When I got home, my sister asked where I had been. She couldn't understand why I had been for a run.

Dad butted in and said: "It's what soldiers do."

Simon hadn't been for a run, but he did ring and ask if I was going into town.

"Yep. See you on the bus."

The rest of my first leave was pretty uneventful. I went up to the Moors and stayed over for a few days, and went for a couple of runs along part of the Lyke Wake Walk.

Once back at Taunton, we had about seven weeks until Christmas.

During that time, we were introduced to the GPMG. There was a barrack range between our accommodation and the Armoury, and three GPMGs lined up on the firing point, with the top covers open. We had fired the SLR and the SMG on this range dozens of times, but now we were in for a real treat.

Sgt. Wilcox and Corporal Glennon had to balance the gun, while Cpl. Ferguson shouted: "EAR DEFENDERS IN!"

The gun was loaded.

Then I heard Cpl. Long shout: "READY!"

Sgt. Wilcox pulled back on the cocking handle, then pushed it all the way forward.

"AT THE TARGET TO YOUR FRONT, IN YOUR OWN TIME. CARRY ON!"

I thought the SLR was loud, but the gun was off the scale!

Before we could fire the GPMG, we all had to pass the training test. We were given a range brief, and told how many rounds we would need. The targets were witness screens, with four white patches; we had to aim at each white patch and fire bursts of up to five rounds. It was only a quick shoot, and we only needed a belt of twenty rounds each; we would fire many more rounds over the remainder of our training. We would also fire the 66mm anti-tank weapon, the 84mm Carl Gustav anti-tank weapon, and the final weapon, which we were trained on toward the end of our training: the 9mm Browning pistol.

Just before Christmas, we went to Tregantle Fort, near Plymouth. It was constructed between 1858 and 1865, as part of a major fortification programme initiated as a result of French re-armament – and it was the spookiest place that I had ever been to. There were rumours that a drummer boy haunted the battlements, and our instructors reinforced these by telling us about their own experiences at Tregantle.

We took over our accommodation, and, on our first night I was chosen, along with six other lads, to do fire piquet, which was like guard duty in the main Guardroom. Armed with pick handles, we started our duty at

1800 hours, after an inspection. It was dark and blustery, and sea mist was coming in from the English Channel. The Guard Commander was Cpl. Long, and he delegated other members of the piquet to various tasks, while I was left in the Guardroom on my own.

Tregantle Fort, near Plymouth.

Opposite the Guardroom was an arch, which led down to what would have been the dungeons; the steps went down into the darkness. I stayed well clear; I kept thinking about this drummer boy.

Soon, my mind started to play tricks on me; I could hear tapping, and immediately thought: *Drummer Boy! He is on the roof!* Well, I wasn't going to go out to investigate.

I went over to the huge, thick oak door, which must have been easily more than six or seven inches thick, with a shiny, immaculate coat of dark-blue paint. I heard the tapping again, growing louder and louder.

Suddenly, Cpl. Long appeared. "You look like you've seen a ghost."

"Thank God you're back, Corporal!" I said. "I can hear the drummer boy; he's on the roof, Corporal."

He laughed and said: "Come with me, dough-bag!"

The tapping I could hear was just rope, rattling against the flagpole in the wind. We all laughed.

The next day was spent on the ranges, then we had free time during the evening. We even got to stay up late. We weren't allowed alcohol, but we had plenty of pop.

Then the singing started.

We all sang "Barnacle Drew the Sailor", "The Engineer Song" and several others, including "Old McDonald" – but all the words had been changed. Proper soldier songs: disgusting! But, what a laugh!

Prior to Christmas leave, we would do our mandatory training objectives of a BFT (basic fitness test), tests on all of the weapons we had been trained on and our APFA test. All of my German class had passed another stage in our German.

Our instructors could see a big improvement in those of us who were left. We had started our basic training in September, with thirty-six of us in 8 Platoon; now, just before Christmas, there were twenty-eight of us left. 6 and 7 Platoon in King's Company would have had the roughly same the same numbers that we did in September, and roughly the same amount of wastage by Christmas. It was the same in Prince of Wales Company, Queen's Company and the two RCT squadrons.

After our Christmas leave we started our second term, which would take us to Easter. The senior platoons in each company and senior troops of each squadron would have their passing-out parade just before Easter leave. There would be no half term; instead, we would have two weeks leave at Easter.

There were more training objectives, such as the CFT (combat fitness test), an eight-mile TAB (tactical advance to battle). During this term, we would also go to Oakhampton on Dartmoor, to complete navigation exercises and fieldcraft objectives. We would also travel to the Brecon Beacons, to be introduced to the Fan Dance. Additionally, we had range days at Sennybridge, to attempt and pass our APWT (annual personal weapon test) on all platoon weapons, which included firing several 66mm anti-tank and 84mm anti-tank weapons. We had been taken into indoor ranges to fire the sub-calibre devices, but now we were firing them full bore. We would also travel to Longmoor Ranges and Training Area for another exercise, learning about entrenchment, defence and other fieldcraft skills. It was a full on, hectic term.

J/LCpl. Paul Davis, 2" mortar training, JSB Taunton.

During this term, Cpl. Savage the PTI said to me, at a circuit training hobby evening: "Why don't you have a go at the boxing evening? Drop the circuit training, 'cos you will do a lot of that anyway."

I agreed, and found myself doing boxing lessons.

No one was unpleasant; every Junior Soldier there was a total gentleman, and became good friends; one or two attended the German classes.

I knew one lad, John Crichton, who was in the Green Howards (infantry). After we had done some sparring, we went to the NAAFI. Iron Maiden were playing on the jukebox, with "Running Free", an awesome record. John mentioned that the band were going to be playing at Taunton Odeon on Saturday 28th Feb (1981); entry was eight pounds. We both decided we wanted to go.

Because it was on a Saturday we had a later night: lights out by 23:00. We could apply for a late pass and, providing we were booked in by 23:30, we would be okay. I asked Sgt Wilcox for a late pass application sheet.

"Here you are," he said, "fill it in and give it back to me tomorrow."

I caught up with John in the NAAFI, who also had a sheet. A question asked the reason for the pass, and we wrote that we would like to see Iron Maiden in concert.

The next day, Sgt. Wilcox signed my pass, stamped it, made a note in his diary, then handed the pass back to me. "Make sure you're back and booked in by 23:30."

"Thank you, Sergeant."

"Are you chuffed, Mark?" asked Paul, later.

"Very!" I replied.

On the day of the concert, I had German lessons in the morning followed by some voluntary work for a local farmer, fixing walls and fences. On returning to Norton Manor, we had tea, then got ready to go and see Iron Maiden. There were no tickets; the eight pounds was payable at the door.

Whenever we went out, we had to wear smart clothes: trousers and a shirt. I mentioned to John that we could wear trousers over our jeans and a t-shirt underneath our smart shirts.

"Good idea," he said.

"Meet you at the NAAFI at 16:45," I replied.

So there we were, in our smart civvies, ready to go and see Iron Maiden.

We walked toward the Guardroom, armed with our late-night passes. We had been paid that Wednesday, and I had fifteen pounds in my pocket. We presented ourselves at the Guardroom and signed out.

The road outside camp was the A358, and it wasn't too busy then. Taunton was about a four-mile walk, but if we got a shift on we could be there on time and still get a hotdog. The concert didn't start until 18:30, but doors were open from 18:00. We ran some of the way and TAB'd for quite a bit of the route.

Cpl. Glennon had mentioned that there were some idiots and thugs who deliberately target soldiers, and they rode around on scooters; we needed to be aware of them. As we passed The Cross Keys pub and continued into Taunton, there was a park, which the river Tone flowed through, as well as a canal with a towpath, from which we could take a shortcut through the gardens, onto a towpath which would take us toward the Odeon. As we approached the path which led to the towpath, John pointed at what appeared to be a group of these thugs. As we made our way toward the towpath, they followed us. We started to walk quicker and broke into a jog. There were only two of us; I counted at least six of them.

They started running toward us, chanting: "SQUADDIE BASTARDS!" One of them shouted: "GET 'EM!"

John and I ran, crossing the canal, and turned left through some park gates. The thugs were about fifty metres away from us, still chasing and chanting – however, they did struggle; a couple stopped, knackered from running, but they continued to pursue us.

Once through the gates, we could see the queue for the Iron Maiden concert. We stopped jogging and casually walked toward the back of the queue.

There was a tall fella in front of us, with very long hair, with some of his friends and their girlfriends; they all had long hair, blonde, brown and black. John asked the gentleman: "Is this the queue for Iron Maiden?"

The fella replied: "Yes, it is. Are you two here to see the band?"

John and I both smiled and said: "Yes, we are."

Just then, five of the thugs came toward the back of the queue. "There's the squaddie bastards!" said one of them, and they quickened their pace toward us.

Then, one of the tall fella's friends stepped forward, along with three other rock music fans – and they were all big lads. Others in the queue saw what was going on and also came to our aid. One fella wore a leather jacket and what I can only describe as a cut-off denim jacket, with a big Motorhead patch on the back. He said: "They're with us. Now run along."

And that is exactly what the thugs did.

The fella with the Motorhead patch smiled and said: "You're dressed very smart."

I looked down and said: "Oh, yes." The fella and his friends then chuckled, as John and I quickly took off our shirts and trousers, to reveal our t-shirts and jeans; we still had smart shoes on, though. We were able to turn our jackets into something to tie around our waists, to carry our smart clobber in.

A blond fella with long hair said: "You must be soldiers."

John replied: "Yes, we're from Norton Manor, in training."

The whole group smiled, and started to talk to us like friends they had known for a long time. They were really nice people, all highly educated – some from the University of Bristol and others from the University of

Exeter. One of them was an accountant, and one was even a teacher. John and I stayed with them for the whole concert.

John informed the group that if it got to 22:15 hours we would need to leave and make our way back to camp.

"O-ten o'clock," one of the ladies said, and they all laughed. "Stay with us; I am sure we can give you a lift back."

We offered some cash for petrol, but they declined, so the least we could do was get them some hotdogs; I needed to feel that I was contributing. The group stuck to their word, and made sure that we were back in camp by 2300 hours.

One of the ladies – a student at Bristol University, studying chemistry – then said: "I didn't want to say anything, but my dad is stationed here. He is the Padre."

They dropped Paul and I off, waved, then were on their way.

The whole experience of meeting that group and watching Iron Maiden was awesome. Everyone at the concert was really nice – and very clever, I thought.

Over the years, I continued to go to see Iron Maiden and Scorpions. Recently, my wife Kerry and I went to see Iron Maiden in Birmingham (17th August 2018), at their "Legacy of the Beast Tour". Dotted along the droves of fans who were going to see the band, the people all had Iron Maiden t-shirts on. It just so happened that it was Bruce Dickinson's 60th birthday – and he is the youngest of the band! I really hope that I am able to jump around like they do when I'm that age.

It wasn't long until Easter, and all the senior intake were in their number 2 uniforms, practicing for their passing-out parade. Our intake had returned from Longmoor Training Area, and most of that weekend was spent cleaning picks and shovels, and coating them in oil. Our gats were spotless.

We were continuing our training programme, with lots of PT, education, weapons training and all the other subjects included in the CMS (Common Military Syllabus). But now there was a big addition: we now had NBC (Nuclear Biological and Chemical Warfare). I found this training incredibly interesting.

We were issued NBC suits ("Noddy" suits). In those suits it is boiling, even on a cold day. Our respirators were issued to us by C/Sgt. (Colour Sergeant) Wilkinson, from the PWO. In the infantry, all soldiers wearing the insignia of three stripes with a crown above them is referred to as "Colour". In the corps of the Army, the same rank insignia would be worn by a Staff Sergeant and referred to as "Staff". On the other hand, a soldier with the same rank insignia in the Household Division would be referred to as "Sir", because of the crown. The respirators were the old S6 type, and we went to get them fitted not in the gas chamber, but in our normal weapon-training classrooms. There was an equalizing valve on the inside of the S6, which should be opened for a second or two, then tightened back up, so that the pressure inside the seal and air pressure outside was equal. Then a chemical which smelt like pear drops was wafted around on cotton wool.

We were each issued a booklet called *Survive to Fight*. This contained all the information one would need to know about NBC – information like how to wear the Noddy suit, how to mask up, the Chemical Safety Rule, how to use atropine, symptoms of this and symptoms of that... It was a very useful book, with text and illustrations.

Part of our NBC practical test included how to go to the toilet; we had to demonstrate emergency urination and defecation – though we didn't go all the way. I'm sure the instructors just wanted to see us throwing "fuller's earth", a beige powder from our DKP 1 and DKP. 2 (decontamination kit personal); DKP 1 was a pad impregnated with fuller's earth powder, while DKP 2 was a puffer bottle. fuller's earth was harmless, and used to absorb any chemical which landed on you. It would get everywhere. When you got it on your face – around your chin, for example – it would draw sweat from you. If you dribbled a little after urinating it would instantly soak up any urine which was dribbled. Quite a lot of troops used it as foot powder, because of its properties for absorbing sweat and other nasty things.

N.B.C. skills were lifesaving, and we all had total confidence in the equipment that we were using. We were shown how to use the NAIEAD (nerve agent immobilized enzyme and alarm detector), which could detect nerve agent and blood agent. It would continuously sniff the air upwind, and alarm troops to warn them that there could be a chemical attack. It could even pick up traces of fly spray two or three miles away – and it worked.

After Easter, we became the senior intake. When we returned after Easter leave, the new intake recruits had already been issued their tracksuits. We were now the sweats of JSB and they were the sprogs.

In an attempt for the sprogs to settle in with kit issue, each Junior Soldier from the senior intake (us) would visit their respective units; the Green Howards and other infantry units visited their battalions; the RCT visited various transport units, then we (the RPC) visited 518 Coy and 521 Coy. We had to travel on the train in our barrack dress, changing at Oxford, then nice coaches were waiting at Bicester train station, to transport us to St David's Barracks.

The first people we met were Cpl. McPhillips (Paddy), who had a strong Irish accent, and Cpl. Hewit, who was a giant. He wore glasses with big, thick lenses, which looked like the huge magnifying glasses; Cpl. Hewit was lost without his glasses. There was a story that when Cpl. Hewit was a Lance Jack (Lance Corporal), some soldiers would tease him by hiding his glasses; he would walk around with his arms outstretched trying to feel for things that he might bump into. Little did those lads know that Geordie Hewit had been to see the optician and been issued with a brand-new pair, so now Geordie had two pairs of glasses. The lads who used to tease Geordie could easy outrun him and jump out of his way – he wasn't built for speed – but he was one of the strongest, most powerful soldiers that I'd ever met. In those days, Geordie lived in a room with two other soldiers. One day, one of them was in Geordie's bedspace, attempting to hide his glasses – little did he know that Geordie was wearing his new glasses. Geordie didn't hurt him much, but he did get a very painful message across to that poor lad.

We stayed at Bicester for one week. We collected our sheets and blankets, then took them to our accommodation. We were then shown around the camp, and identified key personnel within the unit.

St. David's Barracks only had 518 Coy and 521 Coy stationed within, but there were small detachments of other regiments, such as the RMP (Royal Military Police), Royal Signals and WRAC (Women's Royal Army Corps). There were also Pioneers at Simpson Barracks near Northampton, which was the depot and home of the RPC.

Simpson Barracks was also the location of HQ, 23 Group. In April 1993, 23 Group became 23 Regiment RLC and moved to Bicester. 23 Group consisted of 518 Coy, 521 Coy, 522 Coy and 206 Coy.

There were also Pioneer units in Germany – part of BAOR (British Army of the Rhine) – the more notable Pioneer units being:

- 144 Coy WSG and 70 Coy WSG, which were part of 8 Regiment RCT. Portsmouth Barracks, Munster.
- HQ1: BR Corps Defence Platoon, Ripon Barracks, Bielefeld.
- HQ3: Division Defence Platoon, St. Sebastian Barracks in

SOEST, near the Möhne Dam.

7 Platoon, King's Company R.P.C. members.

During our stay at Bicester, we got involved with a lot of digging, and shown how to construct battlefield defences, using concertina barbed wire and six-foot piquets to construct fencing. In addition to that, it was ensured that we had an understanding of the different Pioneer roles and the locations of each unit. Pioneers were part of the security and defence forces in Northern Ireland, at HQ Lisburn, a defence platoon (Rover Group) at Londonderry – not to mention the defence platoon at Kinnegar, Hollywood, near Belfast City, or Harbour Airport (now George Best Belfast City Airport). There were hundreds of Pioneers, and they were all over the world. In all honesty, I never learnt about all of the Pioneer units, but did serve in some.

When we returned to Taunton, we had more training objectives to meet. Two of them were a range camp, followed a few weeks later by our final battle camp, toward the very end of our training. Our range camp included Zeroing and Field Firing, the grenade range and using GPMG in its SF (sustained fire) role. We also had section attack and platoon attack, as part of our fieldcraft.

Our battle camp was more an assessment, or test, of everything we had learnt over our year at Taunton. Our instructors did not neglect us if we couldn't remember things; instead, they coached us through.

Three days before battle camp, we were getting prepared. We packed all our kit in our webbing and large packs, so we were self-sufficient for the first two days of battle camp. We were being airlifted to Sennybridge, and had already had training from the RAF on how to emplane (get on) and deplane (get off). We had even done emergency evacuation of Chinook and Puma aircraft. I was starting to feel like a real soldier!

The first day of our battle camp was upon us. The aircraft eventually arrived at Norton Manor: two RAF Chinook helicopters. We didn't wear any headdress. We had all cleaned our personal weapons and that familiar phrase, "Prepare for battle," was issued by our Section Commanders. Cam-cream went on and we were looking the part. We all knew that this was the first of the six section battle drills, and each one of us had a role to play. One of us was Junior Section Commander, while another was the section 2IC (second in command). I was the section GPMG gunner and my role included navigation, once we deplaned at Dixie's Corner. I had studied my map over the weekend and I had made a route card.

7 and 8 Platoon set up a huge security cordon around the sports field. There were foam fire extinguishers at each end. We could all hear the characteristic sound *("woka-woka")* of the Chinooks' blades as they approached, and a green smoke grenade was lit, to indicate to the pilots the wind direction. We were all in the prone position, as the first Chinook hovered above us. The downdraft was very powerful and dust was flying

everywhere. The Chinook landed and the loadmaster gave one of our Junior Section Commanders the thumbs up, then the first chalks from 7 Platoon emplaned, while the remainder of us tightened up the security cordon. It wasn't long before the first aircraft was ready to take off. Now the downdraft got really windy! Once up in the air, it headed toward Minehead. The second aircraft landed and the loadmaster gave his thumbs up.

When it was my turn to peel off, I picked up my GPMG, folded away the bipod legs, then ran up the ramp into the aircraft, took my position inside, sat down and buckled up. I thought it was surprisingly quiet inside. As the Chinook took off it tilted forward, gained altitude and flew over the Manor House.

When we landed, we had to run down the ramp and take up a defensive position, to form "all-round defence" around the aircraft. I knew exactly where we were, from my own local knowledge of the area, the last two times I had been here. Dixie's Corner was a short TAB away.

Cpl. Fergusson was waiting for us, and said to me: "Which way, then?"

I gestured in the direction and he replied: "Come on, then, let's go."

It was exactly three miles to our harbour area, across a piece of open moorland. It was cloudy but it wasn't raining… yet.

After our final R.V. (rendezvous), Cpl. Fergusson said: "When you think you are there, get the section into all-round defence."

"Yes, Corporal," I replied.

We had about half a mile to go. When we reached a track junction I took out my compass, which I had already pre-set, lined myself up with the direction of travel arrow and off we went. Soon, we met Sgt. Wilcox.

"Well done, lad," he said.

He had already pre-marked where trenches were going to be dug, and it wasn't long before we were digging in. All the skills associated with section in defence were put into action, such as clearance patrols, standing to, range cards, arc sticks and coms cord. Later that night, Sgt. Wilcox delivered orders for an ambush.

He considered it to be an art, setting up an ambush. He particularly liked it when it was sprung; it looked like a Van Halen concert, with trip flares, Schermuly flares and thunder flashes. It took a while to set up, in total silence and darkness.

We all loved the home-run part. There was an urn of tea or coffee waiting for us in a troop shelter, on our way back to our harbour area.

Our final training objective on battle camp was the withdrawal: an eight-mile TAB away from the enemy threat. Our withdrawal was at first light the following Friday; we had been out in the field for four nights.

On our final night, our Section Commander said that an enemy attack was going to happen within the next twelve hours. Our concurrent activity was to fill in our trenches and pack everything; I was nominated as the map reader, though we all knew where the section ERV was. I marked my map with a china-graph crayon and wrote a very basic route card on the back of my range card – it was then checked by Cpl. Ferguson. I set my compass from the ERV to the platoon RV.

Just before first light we were bumped.

"BUG OUT!" shouted Sgt. Wilcox.

The nominated Section Commander took us all to the ERV, did a quick headcount, then said: "Which way, Mark?"

"On me," I replied.

On our way to the platoon R.V., it started to get light. I stopped just short of the R.V. and we formed all-round defence.

Cpl. Long was at the RV. In his wurzel accent, he shouted: "Over here, numb-nuts!"

On our arrival, Lt. Wilde laughed and said to the platoon: "Fill up your water bottles."

We were now on hard standing road, and we fell into three ranks. It was now a five-mile TAB to Dixie's Corner. We were now being led, so I put my map away.

At the end of any exercise, there are always the NSPs and declaration: everyone forms a straight line and points weapons in a safe direction. It is a way of ensuring that weapons are unloaded, clear of ammunition and that all pyrotechnics are handed in. The conducting officer then takes a declaration from everyone, which is: "I have no live rounds, empty cases, pyrotechnics or parts thereof in my possession, sir."

We found ourselves at the HQ and depot of the Prince of Wales Division, while we waited in one of the drill sheds, for road transport to return us all to Taunton. No helicopter ride today; I think the weather conditions put a stop to that: it was claggy and raining, the sort of drizzling rain which just soaks you through to the skin, and you remain wet through. We took the time to repack our personal kit.

When 58 pattern webbing gets wet it becomes heavy, and everyone's webbing and large packs were soaked through, so this was a good chance to empty my large pack and repack. Most of my kit was dry, because everything was individually wrapped in small, plastic bags, all inside a bin liner. I still had two pairs of dry socks, so I powdered my feet and some clean socks, put them on and put my wet boots back on. Most of us only took one pair of boots on the battle camp, because on our return to Norton Manor we would only have two weeks until our passing-out parade. My spare boots were my best boots, all bulled up.

That weekend was spent doing post-exercise admin, cleaning and drying personal kit, cleaning all the platoon's weapons and handing items into the CQMS stores. We were divided into two groups: half cleaned weapons while the other half cleaned G10 stores, like picks and shovels.

This post-exercise admin is what all units do after an exercise, and after operations. It is a pain, but a requirement to maintain, repair and look after kit; all kit needs to be serviceable. We continued to clean kit through Saturday, even after church parade the following day.

Monday was the usual P.T., then we had training tests on each of the platoon weapons, but this time the instructors made it more of a challenge by blindfolding us. We got laughed at, but by the Wednesday of that week we were all successful. There was a reason for us doing the tests: it was a training objective on each platoon weapon system. We were to hand back our webbing to the stores that following Thursday; normally, all weapon training was done wearing webbing. No more weapon training; the only reason we needed rifles now was for rifle and foot drill.

On the Tuesday after battle camp, it was my seventeenth birthday. Lt. Wilde, Sgt. Wilcox and Cpl. Long approached me.

"Birthday today, eh?" said Cpl. Long.

"Yes, Corporal," I said.

Lt. Wilde asked: "What would you love to have for your birthday?"

They didn't expect my reply: "To be a soldier, sir."

Sgt. Wilcox said: "You've already done that, son, you've already done that. Well done."

There was still a lot of drill to do; our passing-out parade wasn't until Friday 24th July. A lot of time was now spent on the parade square, but our drill was now done at company level, with WO2 CSM Callister. There would normally be other platoons and troops using the parade square, and now there were two or sometimes three squadrons or companies square-bashing at the same time. The RSM would usually make an appearance, which was normally in the afternoon, but he would also allocate a morning to each squadron or company. Over the next week, he would get the whole battalion together to practice.

When he shouted out words of command, there was a slight delay before the sound of his voice reached the flanks of the parade. The lads in the middle part of the parade would react instantly, but the flanking lads would react a second later, and for spectators this would be noticeable – a bit like when you see someone kick a football, but because you might be some distance away, there would be a delay before you hear the sound of the ball being kicked.

There were some new drill formations that we had to master. Because of the number of Junior Soldiers, being in three ranks wouldn't have worked; we had to learn our drill formed up in five ranks. This made left and right wheeling difficult, so we needed to learn "forming" both at the halt and on the march – just big left or right wheels, but in five ranks. Everyone in each squadron and company had to work together, and react to executive words of command at exactly the same time as each other.

We also still had other training to complete, such as our education terminal examinations. This was done wearing barrack dress and conducted under exam conditions. We all took Military Calculations and Military Communications; some had an exam in Military History and I, along with fourteen others, had a Speaking and Listening Colloquial German examination, with a native German speaker; we also had to attempt a German written exam.

On Wednesday 22nd July, only two days before our passing-out parade, we all packed our kit. The only things which were to be in our lockers were our number 2 uniforms, best boots, polish and a bull rag, some civvies and our P.T. kit; everything else was in our kit bags and issue suitcases. Today was a big day: the whole battalion was doing dressed rehearsals all day, but now it was with the band of the Royal Irish Rangers. We all had to drink plenty of water because it was a hot day. That night, I fell asleep watching a film in the Globe Cinema.

On the way back to our rooms, we stopped at the WRVS, a TV room with tea and coffee available, inside the NAAFI building. John and the Padre made four brews, and we all sat down on some chairs. The nine o'clock news was on.

The Padre said: "You have both attended circuit training and boxing each week with Cpl. Savage here. I remember my daughter telling me about giving two lads from the barracks a lift back from an Iron Maiden concert, in February – you were both scroats, then; now you both hold the status of 'soldier'. You will need to look after people; you will go to hostile places and meet hostile people, who will be horrible to you. You must bite your lips and swallow your pride, because you're soldiers."

Cpl. Savage added: "Take these with you, wherever you go." He gave John and I a Gideon each. "Soldiers don't fight because they hate what is in front of them; they fight because they love what is behind them."

As soon as I got to my pit, I fell asleep the moment my head hit the pillow.

The next day (Thursday), we were all back in our number 2 uniforms and back on the square. It was probably the busiest day of the week; not only did we have to parade on the square, but we also had to collect all our credits: what money we had saved. For the initial six weeks of our training we would receive £5 pocket money per week; the rest of our wages went into credits. During our second term it went up to £7 pocket money and in our final term we received £10 per week; having completed each term, our wages would increase. The remainder of our wages were saved for us.

Pay parade took ages. We were marched a section at a time to the Company HQ, where CSM Callister was waiting to give us all our credits – the money we had accumulated over the past year – and there was a lot of it.

We didn't have bank accounts – we had to open them once we had left

Taunton, and no banks opened on Saturdays – so we had to take the lot in cash. Each time we got paid we would march into the Sergeant Major's office, one at a time, then state our number, rank and name; the CSM would find our name on his pre-typed list and pay the amount that was next to it.

When it was my turn to get paid, I heard him shout out: "NEXT!"

I marched in: "3156, Junior Soldier Nichol, sir."

He found my name. "Okay, son. Six hundred and seventy pounds. Check it."

I nearly fell over. I counted it and there was indeed £670. I said: "Pay correct, sir." I was rich! I thought that saving £54 for my skateboard wheels only a couple of years earlier was an achievement! I placed the money in the pockets of my number 2 trousers, about turned and marched out, to reclaim my place in the squad.

"NEXT!" the CSM barked.

Once our section had been paid, we marched as a squad back to our block. There were big envelopes waiting for us to put our money in, so that they could be placed in the platoon office safe.

That Thursday afternoon, the CO joined us on the parade square. He inspected one of the guards, then we continued with rehearsals. While we were doing our rehearsals, there were huge tents being erected on the sports fields. Later that afternoon we were sent to get showered, and were allowed to put on our civvies. We didn't have evening meals, because the catering staff had set up a massive barbecue.

Our company instructors and JNCOs arrived in a four-ton truck carrying milk churns full of cider – it had been made at three of the farms where we provided wall-repair help; there must have been twenty churns, each with a tap at the bottom. We were each issued a plastic beaker and invited to help ourselves to the cider; we were on the lash! The cider tasted sweet but not fizzy. It was nice and cool; each churn had formed condensation on the outside.

There were marquee tents and six-foot-long tables and benches. This cider was very nice – and very moreish; we all had quite a few, and there was plenty of it. Our instructors wouldn't let anyone go to bed until it was all gone, because the churns needed to be taken away and refilled, ready for the next day, when all our parents would arrive. Eventually, that night, me and two other lads helped each other back to our rooms.

Suddenly it was 05:30 the following day (Friday 24th July), and we were woken by Cpl. Savage and Cpl. Long barking:

"UP YOU GET, YOU SORRY LOOKING LOT! YOU NEED TO BE OUTSIDE, READY FOR P.T. WITHIN THE NEXT TWO MINUTES! MOVE! … QUICKER THAN THAT!"

We all still had our kit on from the night before; no one had got undressed or made it into their beds the night before. My head was banging as we formed up in our civvy PT kit.

We then went for a run, stopping from time to time to do circuit training. There was a purpose to this:

1. Cpl. Savage wanted to say goodbye. I wouldn't see him for another three years.
2. It was a learning process, so we knew what it would feel like the next day, after a heavy night out on the lash.
3. We were all set, awake and ready for our passing-out parade.

We wouldn't see our relatives until NAAFI break. Until then, we had to get rifles from the Armoury and then a final room inspection. Once our kit was outside, we left our blankets on our bedside lockers and took our sheets to our platoon office, where we exchanged them for new sheets. Our mattresses were checked by the CQMS. We got dressed into our number

2 uniforms, but to limit the amount of walking in our best boots we were allowed to wear trainers. Once outside, we were not allowed back in our rooms. I took one last look at the inside of our hut, which had been home for the past year, then went outside. I would never go back in.

At NAAFI break we met up with our parents. Our personal kit was loaded into cars, then mums and dads were taken for several presentations in the Globe Cinema. The pipes and drums of the Royal Irish Rangers were practicing on the square. I was very happy, but in a way I was also a bit sad; I had my posting order, but I wasn't due to report to 206 Company at Engineer Resources, Long Marsden, and Stratford-upon-Avon, until halfway through August.

Once our passing-out parade was over, we had to collect our envelopes of cash and posting orders. Then we each said goodbye to our instructors; they all shook our hands. As I said goodbye to Cpl. Long and Cpl. Savage, they said: "We will both see you again very soon."

Mum, Dad, my sister and I stayed in Taunton for one more night, before returning to York the following day. We stayed in a bed and breakfast; there were some of my peers staying at the same place.

After a shower and a change into civvies and a pair of jeans, which my parents brought with them, we went to the Cross Keys pub.

There, we bumped into Cpl. Long and Cpl. Savage. "Told you we would see you very soon, Mark," said Cpl. Long.

Mum and Dad were able to call them by their first names, but I still had to call them Corporal – for about ten minutes, until I realized this was just to tease me.

"You can call me Doc," said Cpl. Savage.

"And you know my name," said Dave Long.

Even when we were invited to call NCOs by their first names, we would still maintain the same level of respect for them.

Our parents allowed us to have some beer, but we didn't take advantage – besides, I remembered well only that very morning, this followed an evening of drinking cider; I just had one beer with an evening meal.

There were several other instructors there with their families, and other Junior Soldiers. There was even a Warrant Officer with his son, who had also passed out that day; I knew the WO's son from the German course. He was in the RCT and had been posted to Leckonfield, not far from Driffield in the Yorkshire Wolds, to complete his driver training courses; he had no idea where he would go after that, though we both knew that we would possibly end up in Münster, at some stage soon.

For the remainder of the evening, we all reflected on the past year of our lives. In the background there was a record playing: "Woman in Love" by Barbra Streisand – the very track I heard on my way to Norton Manor, and the last track I would hear as I left.

Robert Ingersoll once wrote:

"We rise by raising others."

Chapter 4

Steve's Joined Up

RESPECT FOR OTHERS is valued by the Army.

> *"No matter what situation you are in, you must show respect and*
> *tolerance for other people, and be able to put yourself in their*
> *shoes."*

We did not go straight home to York; instead, we went up to Farndale. It
was summer, and there were lots of jobs which needed to be done up on
the Dale Head. I walked past and had a look inside the old cowhouse that
Ziggy, Steve and I had kipped in; everything was in order and the yard cats
were on their patrols. I would not see my friends until later that week. Up
on the Dale Head there were walls which needed fixing, from where people
out hiking had climbed over them. There was a door to a barn which
needed to be taken down, repaired, sanded, repainted and rehung on its rail.

The door was fixed and painted by lunchtime the following day, but
new stone needed to be brought by a tractor, along the old railway. It was
a nice, sunny day and I saw people out walking; it was peaceful. *Just like
old times,* I thought. I even saw some of the yard cats – a bit scraggy, but
still catching the odd rodent here and there, then leaving the remains in
someone's porch.

Each morning, I got up and went for a run along the old railway, toward the Lion Inn, then back down toward Farndale for breakfast. My gran made the biggest bowl of porridge I had ever seen, and I struggled to finish it.

She said, in her posh Yorkshire accent: "You were able to eat more than that last year."

This made me think about how my eating habits had changed; I now did not eat half as much as I once did. I began to wonder if I had been greedy before joining the Army. I do not think that I was, but Gran said that I had lost a lot of weight. I think I perhaps got a little bulkier, after all the circuit training Cpl. Savage had put me through.

After my visit to the Moors I returned to York. It was Thursday afternoon and Steve had come to visit me.

Instead of saying hello and how are you, Steve said: "You've had your hair cut."

"Yeah, it is a bit short, isn't it?" I replied.

Steve said: "Will you be going out later? We could go and see if we can get a pint or two in that new pub, recently opened on Clifton Moor. We should get served; we look eighteen."

My mum had put the envelope containing all my money on the table, and I opened it up and emptied it out. Steve just stared in disbelief.

"Is that how much money you get in the Army, Mark?"

I replied: "Yes. There is one week's wages here, Steve." I did not tell him that it had taken me the best part of a year to save it all up!

Steve was stuck for words. Then he said: "Where is the Army Careers Office?"

"I will take you there tomorrow, if you want."

He agreed, and the following day I found myself retracing the route I took when I went for the first time.

In the Careers Office was the Sergeant who had recruited me. He recognized me, asked how I was, then asked if I would mind talking to some candidates in the waiting area: three adults and one school leaver.

Steve sat down and started talking to the potential recruits. He said: "Mark gets paid a fortune."

I warned him: "Don't tell them it is a decent wage you want. Think about what you value. Not things like money, travelling or a brand-new car, but friendship, trust and commitment. Think about your trades, too." Suddenly it dawned on me that I was speaking confidently. They were all listening, including Steve.

I think the young lad and Steve were too old to join as Junior Leaders; they would have to go to other depots throughout the country for their basic training. Adults' basic training was not as long as juniors'; they had an initial five weeks, then further training for their respective trades.

Steve was called to the very same desk that I had been called to. He went for his literacy, reasoning and numeracy test, and within half an hour he was back with leaflets, wondering what trade to choose.

He fretted: "I'm still unemployed. I do odd jobs for people and help to deliver milk, but that's it."

I reassured him: "Once you're in you will love it. You were good at sports in school, so you should be fine."

Steve got his medical appointment just before I started the next phase of my journey. He would still need to attend some sort of selection; he did, however, indicate that he liked the idea of soldiering, and that he would consider one of our local regiments: the Green Howards, Duke of Wellington Royal Regiment, or the Prince of Wales Own Regiment of Yorkshire.

I said: "What did I tell you about the infantry?"

Still, I could not really talk; I was sort of in the infantry. My cap badge had a crown on top, a laurel wreath, a pick, a shovel and a rifle (the tools of the infantry), and at the bottom featured a scroll with the words:

"Labor Omini Vincit" – Latin for *"Labour Conquers All."*

I wanted to go out and buy something goochy; something good, which not many other people had, and I had seen some people walking around with headphones plugged into a portable tape-cassette player. By now, I had my very own Iron Maiden cassette. The album was called *Iron Maiden*; it was released in April of 1980. I took that cassette everywhere I went. I just didn't have anything to play it on; I needed one of these cassette players.

I visited the same shop where I had bought my first disc album *Axe Attack*. They sold lots of music and record players, but no cassette players yet. Dixons did have some cassette players, which were of a suitable size to put in my pocket, so I bought one; now all I needed was the batteries. It took me ages to find two AA batteries, but eventually I found some, in WH Smiths. Once I had power, I was away. I followed the idiot's guide (instructions), placed my Iron Maiden cassette in the player and pressed play. I was sorted.

I played then rewound tracks, to play them over again. I walked through town then back home, playing my Maiden tracks until the batteries went flat.

I was hoping to bump into Ziggy at some stage of my leave, but his dad said that he was away, on a history exchange trip in France, and would not be back until late-August. I would be away by the 15th, so I would not see Ziggy, possibly until Christmas.

On Saturday 15th August 1981 I was on my way to Long Marsden. Travelling on the train was easy now.

I met up with Charlie at Sheffield train station. Charlie had been in 7 Platoon at J.S.B. The train stopped at the usual stations, then on reaching

Birmingham New Street we tried to get a bus, but with no luck. We needed to be at the Royal Engineer Depot by 15:00, and our knowledge of Birmingham to Stratford-Upon-Avon public transport was very limited. Stratford didn't have a train station, but it did have a bus station, where the X50 or X20 bus would stop; we could get either of those two buses from the bus station at Birmingham New Street, but the bus times for that Saturday were cutting it very fine. In the end, we managed to negotiate a £20 taxi ride, all the way to the main gate of the barracks. The taxi driver knew the way, though it must have taken close to 45 minutes to travel to Engineer Resources. We paid the taxi driver and gave him a tip for helping us out.

Charlie and I had all our kit, which included our kit bags, issue suitcases and a smaller holdall bag, and we made our way to the Guardroom. We still did not have identity cards (MOD 90), only our posting orders, but they were enough. The Guard Commander, Cpl. Dolphin, was very slim, with a moustache and a strong Birmingham accent; he was referred to as Brummy Dolphin. He made a phone call to get the duty storeman to issue us bedding.

Our room was on the top floor of A-Block. The entrance had a big, blue sign with a red and green stripe across the middle; *"206 Coy Royal Pioneer Corps"* was stencilled on the sign. The storeman showed us the way to our accommodation, and Charlie and I found that we had a four-man room to ourselves. The storeman left and we unpacked.

About twenty minutes later a Lance Corporal (L/Cpl.) came into our room. Charlie and I immediately stood to attention.

"Please lads, relax," he said. "I am Lance Corporal Bhachu. Let me take you for a look around."

L/Cpl. Bhachu took us on a tour of the barracks, HQ offices, accommodation blocks, fire assembly area, NAAFI and cookhouse. The three of us sat in the NAAFI until 17:00, when the cookhouse opened for evening meals. This was more like a restaurant, with diggers (knife, fork and spoon) laid out on tablecloths and placemats; Taunton had very basic tables with no cloths, diggers or cups. "Bach", as he was known, introduced us to some of the other lads, all Private soldiers (abbreviated as Pte.). Because it was Saturday, later, after our evening meal, they were all going to the local pub in Lower Quinton, The College Arms.

It would have been about 18:00 when Charlie and I walked back across to the NAAFI. The main difference between this NAAFI and the one at Taunton was that this one had a bar, in addition to the normal shop. There was also a TV room upstairs.

Charlie said: "Shall we get some beer, Mark?"

But we were still seventeen years old, and drinking alcohol would be breaking both civil and military law.

Just then, Bach came in. "Drink, lads?"

Charlie said: "Yes, please, Corporal; a pint of bitter, please."

Bach turned to me: "Same, Mark?"

"Oh, er... oh, yes, please," I replied.

I was drinking beer, but I would have been just as happy drinking pop. I think the reason I was drinking it was because everyone else was; I suppose you could say it was a sort of peer pressure – the same sort that young people at school give in to. The beer did not taste bad, it just wasn't sweet, like pop.

As I continued to drink my pint, Charlie issued the odd snipe in his Yorkshire accent: "Hark at thee, suppin' a pint. Come on, Mark, lad, sup thi' pint up."

About an hour later, four of us started to walk toward Lower Quinton; it was about a mile to The College Arms. I must admit I was a bit nervous about going to the pub, but the nerves only lasted for about twenty minutes.

It was almost as if I felt I should only speak when spoken to; at Taunton we were required to address Private soldiers as "Staff".

One of the lads, called Coombsy, got the first round, then a soldier from the Royal Engineers called Sully got the beers in, then it was my turn, then Charlie, then Bach got a round. After two full rounds we had drank between five and eight pints each; this was the most I had ever drank in my life.

There are three villages near the barracks: Long Marsden, Upper Quinton and Lower Quinton. The College Arms, in Lower Quinton, is the closest. It is a sixteenth-century inn which was once owned by King Henry VIII; an old-fashioned pub, on the village green, which soldiers from the Engineer barracks often visit. For quaint and very rural villages, both Lower and Upper Quinton have their share of history.

On St. Valentine's Day of 1945, Charles Walton, a local man who lived near The College Arms, was found murdered; it is believed that the crime happened at Firs Farm, on the slopes of Meon Hill, Lower Quinton. Chief Inspector Robert Fabian led the investigation into Walton's death, but even now the murder has not been solved. Even people who are still around today refuse to talk about the event. He was a 74-year-old farm labourer, known to be a slightly unusual character, although he was well-liked in the village, where he lived with his niece Edie. On February 14th 1945 he was seen trimming hedges on the farm where he worked, and had been witnessed walking to work that morning, carrying a pitchfork and a slash hook, used for cutting branches.

It is said that the Devil was angry about the construction of Evesham Abbey – so enraged, in fact, that he picked up a vast mound of earth and threw it through the air, in an attempt to demolish the abbey. This huge missile was seen approaching by Saint Egwin, who prayed for an intervention; his prayers were so powerful that the huge clump of soil fell from the air, short of the target, to become what is now known as Meon Hill. There are also stories of a black dog on Meon Hill, which heralds death to those seeing it. When Charles Walton was found dead at Firs Farm, situated on the slopes of Meon Hill, witchcraft was suspected in his murder; it is worth noting that Charles Walton was also said to have seen and reported a black dog on multiple occasions nearby. It has even been suggested that the detective investigating the case was a witness to the Meon Hill black dog.

I remember on one occasion, walking from the camp to The College Arms with several lads, we saw a bonfire up the hill. We mentioned this to the landlord, who advised us to stay as a group, and keep together at the end of the night. That night we visited the RBL and The Gay Dog pub, before returning to camp. It was February, it was cold and we returned to camp as a group. At midnight, there was still the fire burning up the hill. When we all returned to camp, we found the Guard Commander reassuring someone who had been chased by some people wearing robes; he had been to see his girlfriend in Mickleton and was clearly in a state of shock.

Years later I was in Belfast, reading an article in a book (from the mobile library) about disappearances of people from parts of the UK; Meon Hill was mentioned several times.

The landlord of The College Arms didn't know the real age of Charlie and me. When he did find out, on Charlie's eighteenth birthday, he said: "So, you and him have been coming in here, drinking beer underage, for ages?"

I said: "Yes. Sorry."

He replied with a laugh: "If you're old enough to have an Army number then you're both old enough to drink my beer. Enjoy."

The tasks that we carried out during working weeks were on the bridging park, ESP (Engineer Stores Park) or at the disposal park, where some equipment was reconditioned and sold off. We had one L/Cpl. called Wally Smith. Wally joined the Army during the days of National Service, when young men were drafted into the forces. Wally was a very patriotic Scot with a very strong Scottish accent, and he was a top bloke. He had served in Northern Ireland, Aden and other operational zones, and had medals which spoke volumes about him. Each day, Wally would march us down to the disposals park. During our mid-morning breaks, Wally would sit and read the newspapers – or, should I say *appear* to be reading the papers – then each afternoon he would march us back to our accommodation. Just inside the main entrance to our accommodation there was a noticeboard, with Part One Orders and Company Orders, and we would all stop and read each set of orders, to find out where on the park we would be working, dental appointments and other vital information that was posted. On several occasions, Wally would ask me if I could see his name printed anywhere. Sometimes, while having a break Wally had also asked me to read the newspaper to him.

A Royal Engineers Warrant Officer noted this and shortly after sent for me. "I've noticed you reading the paper to L/Cpl. Smith," he said.

I replied: "Yes, sir." I explained that Wally would ask me to read orders to him, and I had noticed occasionally other soldiers would ridicule him. "Sir, I don't think Wally can read; he looks at the pictures. When he reads orders, he claims that he has forgotten or lost his glasses – but sir, he doesn't wear glasses."

The WO replied: "Don't be afraid; just ask him."

That night, I plucked up the courage and I did ask Wally if he found it difficult to read.

He went quiet, then replied: "No, I can't read very well. I feel ashamed about it."

I told Bach, who already knew that Wally could not read. From that point on, I would read orders in his absence, and Bach would divert Wally away from the crowd reading items on the noticeboard; I could then inform Wally later if he needed to be anywhere.

His ability to do maths was fantastic, though; he could easily work out height and weight, and do sums in his head to identify total mass and weight, for crane and forklift operators to pick up loads. He could work out time and distance in his head, while the rest of us would be trying to identify what buttons to press on a calculator.

Whenever I read the paper to him, he would stop me and ask questions about the story. I had several books in my locker; I chose one written by the famous vet James Herriot, called *All Creatures Great and Small*, and each night I would read a chapter to him. To help Wally further, I also had the VHS videotapes and some audiotapes, in which Alf White himself was reading the audiobook. Wally found this very useful, because he could rewind and replay. Wally loved the fact that James Herriot (Alf White) was a Scot.

I would like to think that this all helped Wally. He was a soldier and his heart was in the right place.

Charlie and I would eventually go on a detachment to Ripon, where there was an Engineer regiment, at Claro Barracks.

Along the road was a bridging park, where we worked painting and learning how to service bridging, and ensure that all the girders and other components of the bridges were accounted for.

Our accommodation was over the road from Claro, in Deverell Barracks, comprising the wooden spider huts Charlie and I were familiar with from Taunton, the only difference being that we each had our own room. Each wing had partitions, dividing each wing or leg into five rooms, with a corridor along one of the inside walls.

"I'm gonna introduce you to proper beer later, Mark," said Charlie.

Theakston's Brewery was only a short drive away, at Masham. There were lots of local pubs that sold Theakston's and, to be fair, the best bitter did taste nice; quite creamy. I had probably drunk about three pints of best bitter before Charlie thought it would be good to try the much darker Theakston's Old Peculiar (OP); this stuff was much sweeter, and at 5.6% it was pretty strong. It got my attention – and my stamp of approval. These days, people use OP for cooking; soaking meat overnight to marinate it.

On that same night, Charlie said: "Get this down ya."

"Wor' is it?"

"Rum and black," said Charlie.

Later, I remember being in a taxi…

….then someone saying: "Let's put Mark in't graveyard."

And that they did. And they left me there. The taxi driver even gave them a hand to drag me through the gates, propping me up against someone's grave, then leaving me there on my own. They all knew that I didn't like ghost stories or creepy places. They thought it would be a good laugh.

I woke up, freezing cold, to a gentleman prodding me with his walking stick, who was taking his dog for a walk. The gentleman smiled and said:

"Are you okay, young man? I think they were supposed to have buried you yesterday." He smiled and gave me a hand up.

"I'm sorry, sir," I said, "my mates thought it would be a good idea to leave me here. Which way is it to the barracks?"

"Just around the corner, son," the gentleman said, and pointed with his stick in the general direction.

I got back in time for breakfast.

My boss, who was a Captain from the Royal Engineers, happened to be making his way to the Guardroom. I braced up and said: "Morning, sir."

He was laughing more than smiling, and said: "Buggers, aren't they, Mark? Don't worry, we'll get them back."

I said, smiling: "But you were the one in charge, sir."

He replied: "Yeah, I know. It was good, wasn't it? Take the morning off."

I did several detachments while being stationed at Long Marsden. Eventually, Charlie and a section of Pioneers were sent to the Falkland Islands; Lt. Robb was the officer in charge of the detachment.

On April 2nd 1982, a task force was sent to the South Atlantic to liberate the Falkland Islands (Islas Malvinas), South Georgia and South Sandwich Islands from Argentinian forces, which had invaded and occupied the territories, claiming sovereignty over the Falklands and South Georgia, which was and still is British Overseas Territory. The war lasted for ten weeks. From the British forces, 255 were killed, 775 wounded and 115 captured. 649 Argentinian forces were killed, 1,657 were wounded and 11,313 were captured. Three Falkland Islanders were also killed. The Pioneer task was a thankless one: the group of lads and Lt. Robb were sent to retrieve the remains of both British and Argentinian forces; Charlie was part of a Grave Registration Team, sent to repatriate the remains of our fallen. They also had to rebury the remains of both British and Argentinian dead. Charlie was nineteen years old at the time.

I didn't go to the Falklands until ten years after the war, but I did help to load up a container ship called the Atlantic Conveyor, which was a Merchant Navy vessel, and it was huge. The team I was with would escort cement mixers, building materials, five Chinook and six Wessex helicopters on the back of trucks, six GR3 Harrier Jump Jets, and not to mention all the ammunition and explosives which had to be loaded onto the ship; all this equipment was essential for the task force.

Each evening during the war we would listen to the news and latest events. On 25th May 1982 we lost HMS Coventry. The Atlantic Conveyor was also a target, and subsequently hit by two Exocet missiles, which had been launched by two Argentinian Navy Super Etendard jet fighters, killing twelve sailors. All survivors were transferred to HMS Hermes and the ship was abandoned. Then, on 28th May 1982, the Atlantic Conveyor sank while under tow; only one Chinook helicopter was recovered. The loss of the Atlantic Conveyor meant that ground troops had to march on foot across the Falklands, to retake Port Stanley.

The Falklands war came to an end 74 days later, on 14th June 1982, when the Argentine forces surrendered, returning the Falkland Islands and South Georgia to British control.

Charlie eventually returned from the Falkland Islands, but there was no hero's welcome for them; they had to wait 35 years, until 2017, before they received their medals through the post. All the lads that were on the Grave Registration Team returned; I don't know if the task had an effect on their wellbeing, but they all appeared to be okay. That week we went into Stratford-Upon-Avon for the normal Friday and Saturday night beers, and they all seemed fine, even after being exposed to what they had; most people would need counselling and possibly suffer with post-traumatic stress disorder (PTSD), treatment of which would have been in its infancy at that time. I don't think the lads received any treatment or advice back then, but I may be wrong.

Chapter 5

8 Regiment

"Mr. Gorbachev, TEAR DOWN THIS WALL!"

President Ronald Reagan, June 12th 1987.

"Nil sine labor." ("Nothing without labour.")

Royal Corps of Transport motto.

"Labor omnia vincit." ("Labour conquers all.")

Royal Pioneer Corps motto.

We were all living in a period of time referred to as the Cold War. "Cold War" was the term used to describe the state of hostility and tension which existed between the Warsaw Pact (being led by the Soviet Union, now called Russia, and their respective allies) in the East, and NATO (the USA and their respective allies) in the West. It was something we had grown up with and accepted, but as a young soldier I started to learn more about what the Cold War was. I never thought I would be right at the very front of the conflict between East and West.

When World War Two came to an end, in 1945, Germany was divided into East Germany (otherwise known as DDR: the Deutsche Demokratische Republik), with East Berlin as its capital city and West

Germany (FDR: Federal Deutschland Republik), with Bonn as its capital city. I would eventually visit the division between East and West, when I was posted from Long Marsden to Münster.

The process of "Sovietization" was well established, even as early as 1946, in countries which collectively became known as the Eastern Bloc or the Soviet Bloc. The division was an ideological barrier which divided East Germany from West Germany; it was 7000km long. But between 1945 and 1949 there had been no hard or physical border between the two states; up until 1949 it was still possible to cross the border between East and West. It wasn't until 1951 that East Germany began a building program to fortify vulnerable parts of its border, erecting barbed wire, towers, gates and guard posts. Some heavily populated areas fringing the border were cleared of people, and roads, railways and tunnels crossing borders were destroyed, dug up or diverted. The ground near the border was cleared and, in some cases, packed with landmines. By the early 1950s, the border became uncrossable, and the term "Iron Curtain" was dubbed by the former Prime Minister of Great Britain, Sir Winston Churchill. On March 5th 1946, Churchill said: "From Stettin in the Baltic to Trieste in the Adriatic, an iron curtain has descended across the continent."

Churchill's speech is considered one of the opening volleys, announcing the beginning of the Cold War. Dismantling of the Iron Curtain began in Hungary on 2nd May 1989.

The Cold War started in 1945, but had solidified by 1947; it would come to an end in 1991. One of the main events which would bring the Cold War to an end was the Soviet War in Afghanistan, 1979-1989. The conflict in Afghanistan was draining the Soviet economy, eventually forcing the Soviet forces to withdraw. On February 15th 1989, the Soviet Union announced that it would withdraw its final troops from the region.

Casualties, in terms of deaths from the Soviet war in Afghanistan, were quite staggering, with 14,453 Soviet forces being killed, 18,000 Afghan forces killed and between 75,000 and 90,000 Mujahideen forces lost. This war also had the knock-on effect of five million Afghan refugees fleeing the country.

There was also the Chernobyl disaster.

At 01:23 on Saturday 26th April 1986, the no.4 reactor in the Chernobyl Nuclear Power Plant exploded, while a safety test was being conducted. Initially, 30 men died as a direct result of the explosion, but close to 4000 people would eventually die as a result of long-term health issues from the disaster. Approximately 16,000 people in Europe became casualties, but globally it is estimated that there were 60,000 casualties.

As a result, there was civil unrest and revolt in Eastern Europe. Eventually Communist influence in the Soviet Union dissolved, and this brought a change in the Soviet foreign policy, bringing Communism in the Soviet Union to an end.

When the border between Austria and Hungary was opened, these events marked the beginning of the end of the Cold War.

Construction of the Berlin Wall began on Sunday 13th August 1961. The German Democratic Republic (East Germany) started building the wall to prevent Western "fascists" from entering East Germany and undermining the socialist state, though perhaps we all know the real reason was to prevent East Germans from defecting to West Berlin. The Berlin Wall (Die Berliner Mauer) initially consisted of East German troops linking arms around West Berlin, while here and there were dotted barbed wire fences and concrete blocks, called "antifascistischer schutzwall" ("antifascist bulwark"), hoisted by machinery into place. When it was finally completed, the wall weaved its way around West Berlin for 168km.

The Berlin Wall stood until Thursday November 9th 1989, when the head of the East German Communist Party Erich Honecker announced that citizens of the DDR could cross the border whenever they pleased. On that Thursday in 1989, I watched the news from Belfast, of the wall beginning to crumble. Many families were reunited, and I must admit that when I saw these events unfolding on the news, I did have a bit of a lump in my throat. The cruel irony was that, even in the twenty-first century, many Berliners from both East and West Berlin wanted the wall back up.

It was a bit of a shock when I arrived at Portsmouth Barracks in Münster. Our flight took off on a chartered aircraft, from Birmingham Airport to RAF Gütersloh, then a bus took us to Münster.

Immediately on arrival at 144 Company I started to grow up. The Sergeant Major was WO2 CSM Appleyard BEM. He was a Geordie soldier, who reminded me of the RSM at Taunton, who had the same appearance as Battery Sergeant Major Williams from the comedy series *It Ain't Half Hot, Mum*. They all had one thing in common: they were all good shouters.

My new Sergeant Major (or "Uncle Tom") briefed us about discipline, then directed us to the Armoury along the corridor. We were given a kit list, which we needed to have packed that night, because the next day we were going on exercise to Dorbaum Training Area.

I was suddenly wide awake. I was now in 144 Company WSG (Weapon Support Group), 8 Regiment Royal Corps of Transport (RCT).

8 Regiment was a transport regiment, which provided support for 50 Missile Regiment Royal Artillery. On average, 8 Regiment would be out in the field for about nine months of the year, either on site guard, Inner German Border (IGB) patrols or on exercise. Each deployment would normally last for between two weeks and one month.

The kit list I had been given was an "Active Edge" kit list, and all items on the list needed to be packed inside my webbing and large pack. It included spare items of clothing and rations. There were several documents which needed to be kept in the breast pocket of my combat jacket, along with a notebook and a pencil, preferably sharpened at both ends. Everything had to be immaculately clean and serviceable. We were issued our webbing and told to pack it straight away. Later that afternoon, we were allocated to our platoons. I was in 6 Platoon.

I met our Platoon Commander, Lieutenant Starling. He wore glasses, had a deep voice, and was very eccentric and enthusiastic about everything he did. Lieutenant Starling was probably the most intelligent and creative person that I had ever met; being a civil engineer, he had even designed bridges. He was a bit of an envy of other regiments and corps of the British Army. Lieutenant Starling had a finely tuned brain, and very good ideas about solving problems, but was nevertheless the kind of officer who would lead by example; he wasn't afraid to get his hands mucky.

We also met our Platoon Sergeant, Sgt. Fox – a real soldier who displayed the highest of standards and expected only the highest of standards. He was tall, and had a Sheffield dialect to his Yorkshire accent. My Section Commander was Cpl. Pugh, a Scottish gent who was very green – meaning that he wasn't a barrack boy but a total soldier. A bit like the other Section Commander we had, Taff Thomas, he was also a total soldier. My platoon NCOs had all done the infantry Section Commander courses, Junior and Senior Brecon.

They were all the type of squaddie who would book leave, but rather than go home or on holiday, would feel totally at home digging stage-three fire-trenches and living like soldiers for a week or two, practicing section in defence, in the middle of a training area, carrying wooden rifles; they would probably have done a withdrawal and returned to Portsmouth Barracks a fortnight later. They were like the rest of the regiment of RCT and RPC soldiers, who followed a strict disciplined and moral soldiering code; their skills, qualities and knowledge would brush off onto everyone they came into contact with. Each individual formed was an effective team member. They were all stalwart.

We were shown our platoon stores in the cellars, which is where our Active Edge kit would be stored, ready for if Active Edge was called. The store had G1098 equipment, which would also need to be loaded onto trailers and trucks. The equipment in the stores had to be serviceable and, between operations and exercises, we would need to service and maintain the contents of battle boxes, camouflage nets, radios, picks, shovels and other equipment which was vital.

Going to the toilet was very interesting. Each of the ablutions had the normal urinals, and there were three in each toilet. Then there were the cubicles. When I needed to go and "park my breakfast", I was horrified when I opened the door of the first trap; I stopped unbuttoning my trousers and looked at the toilet I was about to sit on. There was a shelf, which would catch your poo, enabling you to inspect your poo, before whipping your arse and flushing the bog! I buttoned up quickly and dashed into the corridor, to get the attention of someone. I found a soldier referred to as Pops Turner – an old and very experienced soldier. I said: "Look in the toilets, Pops; the plumbers have put them all in back to front!"

After one exercise ("Exercise Whirlygig"), the Platoon Commander needed some troops to remain in the field. The end of the exercise (or "endex") had been called, so to avoid all the convoys jamming up the roads, I volunteered to stay out in the field for a further day. I handed in all my ammunition, then made my declaration stating that I had "no live rounds or empty cases in my possession." I was incredibly tired, but at least we didn't need to dig in or dig shell scrapes; it was totally non-tactical – we could even get changed into our tracksuits if we wanted to.

The standard/average German barracks bog.

We were in the woods, not far from the IGB, and we had a campfire. We made a huge garage from two four-toner cam nets, and could even sleep in the backs of the APVs (armoured personnel vehicles) if we wanted to. There was a Shnelly about two miles away that we could use, and we had several crates of Herferder Pils to wade our way through.

There must have been six of us Chunkies and five or six Troggs, all drinking beer, telling stories and singing the odd disgusting soldier song. Despite being tired, I don't think any of us went to our bashas or got into our dos bags. It was good weather, with a cool breeze, and we could see some of the light illuminating the IGB, close to Helmstedt and Alied Checkpoint Alpha.

One of the drivers was Dvr. Phil Ashton. I used to escort Phil, when he was driving trucks all over Germany; we would stay awake for literally days, before being permitted to get some sleep. Phil volunteered to drive the truck and bring Bratty and chips, or Currywurst and chips... ooh, and Herfy beer for everyone. We asked a Pioneer officer for permission and he said: "Of course, but take some lads with you."

We all chipped in 15 or 20 DM each (the Deutschemark, or DM, was the official currency in circulation in West Germany, from 1948 through until 1999, when it was replaced by the Euro). It was enough to feast on and get all the beer.

One of the lads had a radio in an APV, and tuned into BFBS. The first track we heard was "99 Luftballons" ("99 Red Balloons") by the German singer Nina. This Cold War protest song, originally sung in German, was later re-recorded in English. The English and German versions of the song both tell a story of 99 balloons floating into the air, triggering an apocalyptic overreaction by military forces on both sides of the Iron Curtain, each balloon resembling the mushroom clouds of a nuclear blast. To promote the song, the band actually thought of releasing 99 red balloons in Berlin, each containing a dream, to drift over the Berlin Wall. It was a somewhat haunting song, which reminded me of all the reasons I was stuck in the woods in Germany, close to the IGB; we were right at the very front. If the balloon had gone up, the Soviets might have targeted us, possibly with battlefield nuclear devices, death by flash or conventionally (in which case the Soviets would have stormed over the IGB and reached us in five minutes) – either way, life expectancy wouldn't have been very long!

The following day we repaired, patched up and rolled up the cam nets, gathered poles and secured them on the tops of the vehicles. We had to make sure there were no traces of us ever having been there. Our drive back to Münster was direct, meaning we didn't need to follow a battle route, which might have taken all day.

On arrival, I dragged myself to the Armoury. I could hear a radio on, and BFBS (British Forces Broadcasting Service) was playing a track called "Rock the Night", by the Swedish rock band Europe. It had been written by the band's vocalist Rolf Larson (also known as Joey Tempest), in 1984.

It was a catchy tune, which made a person feel alive, and it got my attention. I listened and sang the lyrics in my head, as I walked along the corridor and past the CSM's office.

By now, our Sergeant Major was WO2 CSM Edwards. He was from Grimsby and had a slight Yorkshire accent. He said: "Come on, hurry up. Get yer gat handed in and ger in that bar."

My rifle was gleaming when I handed it in. I made my way toward the stairwell, the CSM still moaning at me because I wasn't going quickly enough.

"Hurry up! Get shit, shaved and showered; you've got ten minutes to get in that bar!"

"Yes, sir," I said.

I was totally knackered. If I'd stopped on the stairs, I think I would have gone to sleep.

Our block had two stairwells; one at each end. I reached the top and went through the swinging double doors, each of which had a frosted reinforced glass panel, which you couldn't see through. Then I turned right and made my way along the top floor corridor, toward my room. Our block had accommodation rooms either side of the corridor, and my room was at the far end.

As I reached the far stairwell, something caught my eye. I looked up to see what appeared to be someone hanging, through the frosted glass panel – my mind must have been playing tricks, I was that tired! I daren't look; I was convinced that someone had taken their own life!

I dropped all my kit, retraced my route and went charging back the way I had already come, suddenly wide awake. I jumped down most of the stairs, then went bursting through the swinging double doors, into where I had seen the CSM.

Luckily, he was still there, chatting away to Lt. Maund. I needed his attention.

"Sir."

No response.

Again: "Sir."

Still no response.

"Sir!" I said a third time. "David!" I shouted.

Now I had both their attention.

The officer said: "He just called you David."

I was going to die.

"Someone's hung themselves, sir," I said.

"Oh, no…" Lt. Maund grabbed his hair in disbelief, then said: "Let's go, Sergeant Major!"

By now, there was an audience in the corridor we were in.

The CSM said: "Lead the way, son."

"I will phone the Medical Centre," I heard one voice shout out.

I led Lt. Maund and the CSM up the stairs. By the time we reached the top floor, I could see medics running toward our block with a stretcher and medical bag. We walked along the corridor to the far stairwell. I looked down, covered my eyes and gestured by pointing: "In there, sir."

"Shit," I heard him say. He looked and walked toward the door.

By now, the CO and MO, plus three medics, were through and onto the corridor that we were on. The CSM opened the swing doors.

"Oi, come here, numb-nuts!"

I walked toward him, peeping through my fingers.

I was relieved to find that it wasn't someone hanging, but a German painter and decorator on a step ladder, painting the ceiling with a roller.

The CSM and the rest of them burst out laughing at me. Even the CO, Lt. Col. Barlett, couldn't stop laughing.

The CSM, still hysterical, said: "Get a shower and get in that bar…

yesterday!"

I felt like a real fool, but I learned something that afternoon. The CSM didn't go mad at me, but he could quite easily have done so; I learnt that to become a Sergeant Major you need to care – and the CSM did indeed care.

Eventually, I walked into the bar. The CO was there, still laughing, and I could see the shoulders of everyone else going up and down as they chuckled. The CSM ruffled my hair and said:

"Get me, the CO and the medics a beer! You gave us all a heart attack!"

I didn't get any extra duties; I just got laughed at by everyone. Though the CSM did say that I had to babysit for him, to redeem myself.

Each exercise or operation followed a similar pattern: we provided protection for the drivers and security for the custodial items they were transporting. Each time we reached a location, we would clear the woodland, then set up a security cordon for trucks to stop and for drivers to rest. We never remained in any location for more than 72 hours. We would occupy defensive positions, and very often we had live ball ammunition. If we were issued ball ammunition, we knew that whatever was in the containers was live. Very often, we would have a Polizei (German police) escort to take us through traffic lights, and occasionally we would be transported by aircraft, usually in the form of a Chinook helicopter.

Sometimes I was taken away from the section. I wasn't bad at speaking and listening in German, so I could be used to translate for the OC or the CO. It was a cushy number and a good job to get, because I would get a nice, warm truck to sleep in, while the troops were wet through, stood in trenches. I would also be sent to visit previously used locations, to tidy up and collect any items that exercising troops had lost. Sometimes, we would find starred items or restricted documents, left behind by troops. Normally, in a defensive location, soldiers would use minimal equipment, in an attempt to reduce the risk of losing stuff. We would gather up what we found, label it and return it to the various units.

The clearing up task had to be done, and there was a good reason for it: "SOXMIS" (Soviet Military Mission in Western Europe). Often there would be SOXMIS vehicles, normally coloured black, containing Soviet troops, and sometimes with occasional Spetsnaz (Soviet special forces) attached to them. They would look around locations which had been occupied by NATO troops, and were legally allowed to do this; SOXMIS was legal spying.

There was a detachment of RMP (Royal Military Police) – nicknamed "White Mice" – tasked to monitor SOXMIS activity, themselves in cars which were also nicknamed "White Mice". Across in East Germany, we had a similar organization called "BRIXMIS" (meaning British Commanders'-in-Chief Mission to the Soviet Forces in Germany).

SOXMIS and BRIXMIS were formed with the Robertson-Malinin agreement, on 16th September 1946. SOXMIS and BRIXMIS would identify each other's exercising locations, to rummage around and try to find useful information, then pass that information up to respective Intelligence units. SOXMIS had its offices in Bünde.

If ever we saw a SOXMIS vehicle, our immediate action was to try and stop the vehicle, then place blankets over the screen so that they couldn't take photos of our convoys of tanks – in particular the Challenger Main Battle Tank. Then, once convoys had passed we would release SOXMIS. We also had to inform a liaison office in Herford at the earliest opportunity, but we couldn't do this until we had access to a phone; no mobiles in them days. All British Forces were issued a card containing instructions. All SOXMIS vehicles had a yellow registration plate with a number that had to be recorded, along with the location of the sighting.

BFG FORM 66 (Rev Jun 86)

SOXMIS

THIS IS A
TYPICAL SOXMIS
NUMBER PLATE
REMEMBER
The number will be
different on each car.

SOVIET MILITARY
MISSION - BAOR

If you see a SOXMIS vehicle, contact as quickly as possible.
HERFORD Mil 2222
If using a German Civil Phone dial
a. In HERFORD Code 89 then 2222
b. Elsewhere Code 05221-89 then 2222

Figure 1 SOXMIS card issued to all NATO personnel.

SOXMIS were very interested in the role of 8 Regiment, and they would, from time to time, have an East German officer with them. If I was lucky, he would wind down the window and allow one of us to talk to them – which was usually me. SOXMIS would try to find any useful information, such as radio frequencies and coding systems. If war had broken out, all members of 8 Regiment would be prone to capture, because of the nature of our role, so we had to ensure that locations we had occupied were left with no trace of us ever having been there.

There were special courses available to soldiers who had a role like ours, such as LRRP (long-range reconnaissance patrol) training, which was open to all NATO forces. Though the course was in its infancy, some Pioneer soldiers, including myself, found ourselves on the LRRP school. This was done in Bavaria and the Hertz Mountain, and it was freezing; I had never been so cold in my life! Additionally, most of the course was outside. The course was a pre-requisite, meaning that we had to do it before being selected for the BRIXMIS mission.

Service personnel were required to be steadfast, resolute and committed. At that point in my life I had met several members of BRIXMIS, and one thing that made them stand out was that they were all friendly, approachable, amazing people. They never bragged about what they did; they swallowed their pride.

BRIXMIS had a Mission House in Potsdam, just southwest of Berlin, on Seesraße; it was a big, white building which resembled a mansion house. There was a Union flag on the roof and gardens at the rear of the Mission House, which reached as far as the Heilinger See. Very often there would be seen rowing boats, with two occupants – one rowing and the other clearly taking photographs, with cameras featuring high-powered lenses. They were Stasi, East German secret police.

The Stasi were a hated organization, and part of the East German government. The Stasi didn't have any formal role, but they were responsible for domestic political surveillance and foreign espionage. Families might live unaware that their mum or dad, brother or sister were possibly members of the Stasi.

For BRIXMIS to get to the Mission House from West Berlin, they needed to cross the Glienicker Brück. This bridge was also known as the "Bridge of Spies", where political prisoners and spies were exchanged, and is the subject of the documentary thriller film *Bridge of Spies*, starring Tom Hanks, which is based on true events.

BRIXMIS had a very challenging role. They didn't have political immunity, though they did have some immunity. Their vehicles were highly tuned and race-ready.

BRIXMIS card issued to Warsaw Pact troops.

Eastern Bloc troops were issued a card similar to their British counterparts', so that they could report sightings of BRIXMIS. The Soviet forces were very aggressive toward the BRIXMIS Mission, and would often ram their vehicles off the road, or deliberately scrape the side of

BRIXMIS cars with armoured vehicles; BRIXMIS troops were often detained by Soviet forces. BRIXMIS was a mission with its dangers, and there was no safety rope; detainees were on their own, surrounded by hostile forces.

BRIXMIS did some amazing missions. They would rummage around in what had been latrines for exercising Soviet units. We were issued toilet paper that we nicknamed "John Wayne", because it was rough and tough, and it didn't take no shit; it was like tracing paper and, rather than comfy, it was prickly. Soviet soldiers didn't get issued any toilet paper, so they would use anything they could get their hands on, such as paperwork like receipts or pages of books. But sometimes the BRIXMIS lads would strike gold, and find screwed up radio documents, containing coding and decoding information which was very valuable to our intelligence sections. The BRIXMIS mission also found plates or explosive reactive armour, which was considered top secret to the Soviets, but gave our forces a good idea of what the Soviets were using to protect tanks and tank crews; this would prime the West to develop anti-tank weapons which could penetrate the armour. BRIXMIS missions took incredible bravery.

One such mission was done during the Soviet war in Afghanistan. Injured Soviet soldiers weren't "cas-evacced" (casualty evacuation) back to the Soviet Union, but were taken to hospitals in East Germany. BRIXMIS had a mission to visit these hospitals, which didn't have high levels of security. If Soviet troops needed amputations, the amputated body part would often be thrown into a skip, ready for incineration. After their surgery, the troops from BRIXMIS would wear NBC (nuclear, biological and chemical warfare) gloves and fuller's earth to protect themselves, then find and retrieve body parts like arms, hands, feet or even legs in these skips, usually wrapped in a plastic material. BRIXMIS would remove these parts from the skips and place them in sealed containers, ready for transportation back to Berlin for analysis. Later it was discovered that Soviet forces may have been using chemical weapons against the Mujahideen and other insurgents. It may have been carelessness by Soviet forces – using artillery shells or aerosols, without checking the weather conditions for wind direction – which resulted in them contaminating themselves with damaging agents, like blister agent.

A BRIXMIS senator about to cross the Glienicke Bridge, 1986.

BRIXMIS was a detachment which really appealed to me, and I wondered if I had the qualities and skills needed for such an awesome mission; I felt that BRIXMIS was a role I could apply myself to. I could even identify some of the dialects that were close to the IGB region. They were much like accents we have in the U.K.; for example, a northern accent and southern accent sound clearly different, but even in the north there are differing dialects. A person from Leeds sounds different to someone from York; both have a Yorkshire accent, but the dialect differs. When Arnold Schwarzenegger, who starred in the film *The Terminator*, speaks English, he has a German accent, but when he speaks German, his accent will differ from someone from the northern part of Germany. Additionally,

Schwarzenegger is from Austria, one of the German-speaking nations within Europe, so his accent also differs from a person who comes from München (Munich). Arnold Schwarzenegger wanted to remake *The Terminator* in German, but the producers rejected the proposal, because Schwarzenegger's accent and dialect would have sounded like a country accent in Germany; *"I'll be back!"* wouldn't have quite the same impact.

Travelling to Berlin was quite interesting; we could go by aircraft and land at R.A.F. Gatow, West Berlin, though my favourite route was the BMT (British Military Train), called "The Berliner". There was also the cheap option of travelling by road. I never flew, but I did travel on the train to Berlin twice. The duty driver or a garrison driver would take us to Hanover train station, where we would board The Berliner; we had to have the relevant paperwork, such as identity cards and a NATO travel order, available and ready for inspection if requested.

The RCT's very useful propaganda tool was a train; I had never been on anything like it. The Berliner was like the Orient Express; there was a restaurant carriage, the carriages passengers travelled in were ornate with gold-plated bits and bobs, and there was a lovely smell everywhere on the train. There were even staff to help you order beer and wine. Each carriage was called forward, one at a time, to visit the restaurant carriage, to enjoy an a la carte menu. Everything on The Berliner was first class.

The train would leave Hanover and start heading to Braunschweig station, not far from Helmstedt, on the IGB. Then there was normally a delay, while the engine was changed at Braunschweig. At one end of the platform (gleis), there were representatives from the British Army (normally an RCT officer or WO) and two SNCOs, one of which spoke Russian. At the other end of the platform there were the Soviet equivalent of ranking officers and NCOs. They would turn and face each other, march toward each other and halt at the middle carriage; both officers would then salute each other and exchange documents, before the Soviets would board the train and inspect our documentation. There would be dog handlers and what appeared to be Soviet infantry patrolling – not to stop people leaving the train, but to stop people getting on. Once paperwork was checked, we would be on our way through the Berlin Corridor.

It was like stepping back in time. East Germans would always go to the level crossings, to wave at passengers on The Berliner, and were very often monitored by Stasi and Soviet forces. They would stare at the train as it passed, and we would see lines of Trabant or Wartburg cars, which the average citizens would drive around in. Most of the trains we passed along the Berlin Corridor were old, post-WW2 steam trains, with very basic passenger carriages. The Berliner was a propaganda tool intended to impress the Soviet forces and East Germans, to make them think that we lived like kings and queens.

Having eventually arrived at Charlottenburg train station, we would then be on our way to our respective units.

Another way to travel to Berlin was by car, along an autobahn, and there was a series of checkpoints to go through. At Helmstedt there was a prefabricated building called "Alied Checkpoint Alpha", and along a narrow corridor was "Soviet Checkpoint Alpha". Everyone had to file past each reception, where paperwork and identity cards were checked by the American Military Police or the RMP (Royal Military Police), before going through to the Soviet military. Having checked in, you would re-join your vehicle, and you then had two hours to reach the next checkpoint (Soviet and Alied Checkpoint Bravo), though you had to keep to the speed limit; if you were too early, the Soviets would charge you with speeding. But you couldn't go too slow, either, because if you were too late you were charged with espionage. The whole autobahn was heavily patrolled by the East German police and the Stasi. And there were also Soviet officials, always watching.

Twenty-seven years later, in 2010, Kerry and I visited Münster and Berlin. Arriving at what was Portsmouth Barracks, I couldn't believe how much the trees which lined the main road through my old barracks had grown; they were huge!

Portsmouth Barracks had four accommodation blocks, a NAAFI complex with a shop, an HQ building which housed the RQMS stores, which then joined onto the Warrant Officers and Sergeants' Mess. There was a vehicle park for all the trucks and Land Rovers, a parade square and, eventually, a brand-new cookhouse. In addition, there was an obstacle course, gym, a small chapel and several other small buildings. The main gate held a guardroom, which had several cells for soldiers under sentence.

The main gate led out of the barracks onto Edelbach, while the pedestrian gate at the opposite end of the barracks led out onto Hohe Heckenweg. The Hohe Heckenweg gate was the one we would use to go into town, or along the road to the bar which most 8 Regiment troops used, The Coerde Krug. We would travel along Hohe Heckenweg toward town, taking the number 8 bus to Prinzipalmarkt, just by St. Lambert's Church, or the number 10 bus to the Hauptbahnhof.

Hohe Heckenweg had a families' NAAFI, the officers' mess and several areas designated as married quarters. The name "Hohe Heckenweg" means "path of high hedges", and there were several high hedges, including what appeared to be an avenue of poplar trees, on both sides of the road. The barracks are now known as "An Der Meerwiese" ("At the Sea Meadow"); all the buildings are now residential flats.

As we walked past what was the NAAFI, something sent a chill down my back: we could hear some music coming from one of the apartments, and there was a small child, probably about six years old, standing on the balcony: the song was "99 Luftballons" ("99 Red Balloons") by Nina. It was one of the first tracks I heard on my arrival in Germany, on the radio back in 1983. Now, some 27 years later, I was listening to it again.

The main road through Portsmouth Barracks, looking toward the back gate.

Chapter 6

The Good Old Padre

"Even a Padre can fight a war."

Andrew Nichol.

Even my normal role in the gym would require me to join my normal section in 144 Company. During "Exercise Lionheart" I was required to speak some German for the officers who needed help. I was part of a section selected to provide protection for Gen Walker, the GOC 3 Division for Exercise Lionheart, September and October 1984. This exercise was the largest movement of troops since World War Two, and there were around 130,000 members of the British forces taking part, from the regular and territorial services.

I had been in that trench for a few days, having had to move my position ten metres to take advantage of cover; being closer to trees, foliage and branches would provide me with the cover I needed, and I had a better field of view. Well, that's what I thought, anyway.

The real reason was awful. We had arrived at this location the previous week, to prepare a defensive position. Because we were there for more than two days, we needed to dig stage-three fire trenches. We had arrived under cover of darkness, and managed to establish a harbour area.

There were several vehicles. Ours was an APC (armoured personnel carrier), a 432 tracked vehicle which the Irish Guards had loaned to us. It was called "Askeaton", named after an ancient town on the banks of the Deel River, in County Limerick. Askeaton had a B.V. (boiling vessel) unit, which could be used to boil water for hot drinks, and there were also cages inside the vehicle, making it easy to store equipment. My seating position in the vehicle was directly behind where the Commander would be.

As soon as we deployed from Askeaton, we formed all-round defence and carried out clearance patrols. It would only be another hour and a half until first light, so we needed to have established ourselves as much as we could. We estimated that we only had one more week on exercise, and we were all looking forward to endex (end of exercise). Gus showed me where I needed to dig my trench. It was still dark, and I started to remove all the topsoil from where my trench would be dug. Gus had said to me that the whole harbour area was very smelly, but my sense of smell isn't all that good, so I couldn't smell anything. It would have been between 04:00 and 05:00 now, and I estimated that I could have at least started my trench (there appeared to be a ditch that I was able to shovel soil into), but only if I got a shift on. I was quite lucky considering I was between two pine trees; there were hardly any roots, so digging was easy. After about a foot in depth, I started to hit stones and boulders. The length of the trench and sleeping bay was about nine feet, and I could start to see the outline as we reached "stand to".

Stand to would be carried out from half an hour before first light until half an hour after first light; the length of time would depend on what the Platoon Commander wanted. Stand to was also done in the evening, as the sun was going down. Everyone occupied their defensive positions and waited in their fire positions until "stand down" was given, at which point the section would go into either daytime or night-time routine.

Once the term "stand down" had been issued, I continued to shovel stones and pick out boulders with my hands. It was hard work digging the trench. I was soon down at knee-depth, at which point Gus came and he had a hot drink for me. When someone makes you a hot drink, your morale shoots up. Gus handed over the brew, then said:

"Mark, it really does smell of shit over here! Over there, too, but it is much worse here."

There was limited light, because of thick foliage, but Gus told me to stop digging for a second. He had a red torch, and when he shone it there was screwed up toilet paper and human waste everywhere. I had been digging in a latrine! Two weeks previous, the German Bundeswehr had occupied that same position, and where I was digging had been a latrine; I was literally covered in shit.

Gus was busting to laugh, but thought better of it, and even appeared to be sympathetic. I had to fill in the trench I had dug, while Gus chose another position, a bit farther out. That was fine, because we could drop back during the night. It wasn't just me that had dug in a shit-pit – others had, too – so I wasn't the only one who would be laughed at when the General came to visit. The General dropped in by air, in a Gazelle helicopter, then he would disappear then return – it was like that for several days.

The whole position was quite big, and there were Royal Signals Control Posts and wagons here and there; we even put up several 12 x 12 tents, where the GOC could give briefings. There had been previous locations where the GOC and ourselves had been, in barns and part of a factory complex. I could hear generators humming away, and from time to time I got the smell of the food being cooked in the field kitchen. The chefs needed tents, so we put up their tents, too.

Roles within sections can change, and my role within the section now was as the 84mm gunner. My personal weapons (yes, plural) were the Carl Gustav 84mm anti-tank weapon and a 9mm Sterling submachine gun. All

Active Edge (webbing and large pack) kit had to be inside the trench; weapons had to be functional and gleaming – which was a little difficult in muddy conditions. If a weapon was dirty then it might not function; there might be a stoppage.

We were way up in the north part of Germany, not far from Lübeck. Our position was on a hill, with a shallow slope toward the edge of some woodland, overlooking a small town. The weather was overcast and there was a bit of rain; inside the wood we were in it was fairly dry, but it had been raining the day before. I liked the idea of the chefs being there; we would often get a brew, because they had hot water on the boil all day and all night.

It was Friday morning at about 05:30, during stand to, when we heard a siren coming from the local town, then an almighty bang. Immediately we got down in our trenches, with our steel bongies (helmets) on our heads. The bang was a simulated nuclear explosion, which had been mentioned in our "O group" (orders/briefing). The immediate action in the event of a battlefield nuclear attack was to get down, until both the positive and negative waves of the blast had passed.

About one hour after the first siren we heard another, which signalled "all clear". In reality, after a nuclear strike the siren would fail to function.

By now, I had swapped weapons for the day; I now had my old friend the GPMG, and a belt of 200 blank rounds, pointing in the direction of the enemy threat. I could hear some chattering, so I made sure stuff was secure and kit put away, just in case we needed to withdraw. There was no rubbish left; my trench had puddles, but it was spotless.

Suddenly, the GOC, the CO of 8 Regiment, the Padre and my Section Commander Corporal Gus Patton came across to my trench.

Gus said: "This is Private Nichol, sir; the smelly git."

The CO always wore a Pioneer beret with an RCT cap badge. He was smiling when he spoke: "Hello, Mark. How are you?"

I replied: "I am fine, sir, but you all need to get in my trench; there's enough room. Come on in."

Everyone got into my trench, including the Padre, who held the rank of Major.

"So, you're Mark?" he said. "The one who was covered in the brown, smelly stuff?"

I replied: "Yes, Padre."

The GOC said: "Come on, Mark, out of your trench. The CO and Padre have some beer back in Münster, and some of the bottles have your name on them. Endex was called over an hour ago. Come on, son."

I felt good, and quite important – all because the General and the CO used my first name. It was like I had made a big contribution; that felt good.

I didn't realize at the time, but the Padre was on a recce; I wouldn't find out about it until I returned to Münster. Even then, it was nearly two months before I saw the Padre again.

One morning, we had attended the Remembrance Parade, and now all units were completing IGB patrols and getting ready for site guard. I had completed cross-country running training, when the Padre appeared and said:

"I might have a job for you, when we return to Münster."

I did catch up with the Padre, who was a very kind and caring person. I made a nickname for him, by way of teasing him; I called him "Your Holiness". He laughed, and thought it was a good name to have. Going to the gym each day was my normal work routine, but I made time each day to go and make him a cup of tea, and from time to time we would see him in town. He was about ten years older than Charlie and I.

While walking to share a taxi with him one day, he said: "What do you know about evil, lads?"

Not being much of an intellectual, I said: "Evil is when bad things happen, Your Holiness."

He told me: "Elaborate, Mark... Charlie, tell Mark what it is."

Charlie pointed at a homeless person and said, "That is evil: hunger, thirst, nowhere to live and no money."

Evil manifests itself in different ways. Some people form their image of the Devil as a figure with red skin and a pointed trident, bathing in fire. On this occasion evil had manifested itself as Charlie had indicated, when he pointed at the homeless person; it wasn't the person who was evil, but the situation that he was in. Plague, pestilence, famine and war are all evil.

The Padre went on to say: "It is up to the soldiers of God to confront and fight evil. Be soldiers of God."

It was almost Christmas, and the Padre was preparing the choir; on the run-up, he often had choir practice with some of the German locals in the gym. I don't know what it was, but although I like my heavy rock music, I also enjoyed listening to the choir doing their practice. Even now, thirty-six years later, I listen to our school choir when they practice. Now we are in 2020, I don't know if they will get to practice this year, due to the new invisible enemy SARS Cov 2, the virus which causes the disease CoViD 19. At this moment, in 2020, it has become a global emergency.

Each year, the regimental choir would sing in St. Lambert's Kirche (church) and at St. Paulus Dom (cathedral). About one week before Christmas, the choir would do rehearsals at both churches and, if I was with the lads in town, I would claim that I needed the loo and would meet them in one of the bars – but really I wouldn't go to a loo; I would go and stand outside the doors of each church, listening to all the choirs. After about an hour I would be freezing, so I would go and find the lads, and have a beer.

On several occasions, there had been a homeless fella with a sign in front of him, reading: *"Ich habe hunger" ("I am hungry")*. I did notice him twice, and the Polizei (German police) hadn't shooed him away. On other days I would see the man sat close to the dom, hopeful that he might be lucky and thrown some loose change by people leaving. One night, I went into town with Charlie and two other lads. Charlie had missed his evening meal and was peckish, so we got a burger meal each at McDonald's. I told Charlie about the homeless fella, who was in his usual place. Charlie and I approached him near the dom, and handed over a Big Mac meal and a coffee. I was able to hold a conversation with him – he struggled when speaking, even though he had a loud voice – and found he had been in the German Army, or Bundeswehr, as a "Halb Gefreit" – the equivalent of a Lance Corporal. He had been stationed near the training area at Dorbaum, as part of a tank or panzer crew, but had been badly injured and needed to be discharged on medical grounds. When he got up to walk, he needed a helping hand; but he needed far more help than Charlie and I could give him: he needed support from his former employer.

The three of us could hear the choir, and we listened until they had completed their rehearsals. I felt mean when Charlie and I left, but I explained to the man that we would see him the following day. Then we walked away to join the remainder of our group. After that, I had a sort of haunting feeling, which stayed with me all night and through to the following day, which was Sunday.

That weekend, the Padre had been in the dom, performing in front of an audience. On the Monday, the Padre sent for Charlie and I; he had tea, coffee and biscuits. Charlie didn't like hot drinks, so he settled for orange pop.

The Padre said: "The 2IC (Second in Command) of the regiment saw you two near the dom and St. Lambert's over the weekend; you'd given someone some food... a McDonald's meal, I believe."

"Yes, Padre," I said, "sorry."

He frowned: "Why are you sorry?"

I said: "Dunno, Padre."

"We can never solve the problem of homelessness," he said, "but we might be able to point these people in a promising direction."

He gave me a card, to give to the man if we saw him again; it was for a German charity, which provided support for the homeless. Charlie mentioned to the Padre that the fella may have felt abandoned, and the Padre agreed.

He said: "Have you ever heard of a floating coffee?"

Charlie and I both said no.

The Padre continued: "It's a place where people can donate to any of several coffee shops in Münster; the idea is that each coffee shop receives enough cash to pay for a hot drink for anyone they wish, like old people, the homeless and beggars."

"There we are, Padre," I said: "even you can fight a war."

The Padre's idea was to use this model with the main NAAFI family shops – almost like supermarkets, where customers receive tokens; how many tokens the customer receive would be dependent on how much they spend. He wanted it to happen at our families' NAAFI.

"You have both inspired me to motivate myself," the Padre said.

Only a day or so before Christmas, the Padre had generated nearly 350 DM (Deutschmarks) to distribute between three coffee shops. Each families' NAAFI had received donations either in collection boxes or stamps, a little like "Green Shield" or "Saver" stamps, which were then converted into cash for the three coffee shops. It continued well into the new year and summer.

"How do we inform the homeless people?" I asked the Padre, later.

"This is where you two soldiers of God come in," he said. He gave

Charlie and I a stack of tickets, which when translated read:

"Present this coupon at Charlotte's Coffee Bar, Alligator Bakery or Münster Bahnhof Coffee Bar, and you will receive a free hot drink and a pastry."

That haunting feeling I'd had was going away. All Charlie and I had to do was distribute the coupons to any homeless we saw. This would only happen during the colder months of the year, but donations were collected from each of the NAAFI shops throughout the whole of each year. And it wasn't just Charlie and I distributing coupons; there were lads from other barracks in Münster issuing the same tickets. I liked this idea of a "floating coffee", even just during the winter months; at least the homeless people in Münster would receive one hot drink a day.

Chapter 7

PTI

"No man's brain is at its best unless he is physically fit."

Field Marshal Law Montgomery KG, GCB, DSO, PC, DL.

DISCIPLINE is an Army value.

The Army has to be a disciplined force, so every soldier needs to follow the rules and be responsible for themselves.

Margaret Thatcher once said:

"Discipline yourself to do what you know is right and important; difficult is the high road to pride, self-esteem and personal satisfaction."

There had been two of us training to become PTIs while in 8 Regiment. I had worked in the gym, along with all the other PT instructors, for about three months, before attending my course at the Army School of Physical Training in Aldershot. We had instruction every day on how to take recruits PT and trained soldiers PT, and I had learnt how to conduct all the annual and biannual tests and assessments, which all soldiers had to complete.

I wasn't bad at gymnastics, either. I had to learn a routine on the trampoline, and be able to demonstrate perfect vaults and a handstand, then exercises such as rope climbing, pull-ups (heaves), sit-ups, push-ups and all the other exercises associated with the various tests. The only thing I was in need of was boxing and basketball training; I had to learn the rules, how to referee, take scores and judge in each of those two sports.

The boxing was straightforward. I was put in the company boxing team. I had three bouts, won two and lost one. The whole experience of the boxing team reinforced self-discipline, and all the boxers from the sub-units of 8 Regiment were total gentlemen; we even did some of our training together.

Everything I needed to know I learnt in my pre-training. I had already represented the regiment, the Army and BAOR for several years, at cross-country running in the winter months, and the 1500 metres and 3000 steeplechase during the summer months.

We had successful teams in all the sports the regiment had to offer. Training for events and training in general can become obsessive, to the point that we would train several times each day. On occasion we might miss a day of training, and whenever this happened we would have a feeling of guilt. Normally, Phil would come across to our block at daft o'clock in the morning, I would get changed and we would go and train, whatever the weather.

As a warm-up for cross-country training, we would play basketball with the regimental team – which was good for me, as it provided me with the knowledge of the sport that I needed. The regimental basketball team would always thrash us. We would then go for a run, concentrating on different aspects of running: for example, running up a hill isn't hard; it's the 200 metres after you reach the top, trying to get back into your original pace, that was the killer – I would be breathing through every orifice, trying to regain my pace.

Our catering officer was Lt. Price. He was a tall gentleman, married and living in married quarters, over the road from the back gate of Portsmouth Barracks. Lt. Price was like a friend; he was an officer, so we totally respected his rank, but he allowed us to call him "Sir Bob". Sir Bob trained us hard, and we would reap the rewards every Wednesday, at the 3rd Armoured Division Cross-Country League Championship; we won most, if not all events, for three successive years. Our main rivals were 50 Missile Regiment Royal Artillery and the 1st Battalion Irish Guards, though the Guards did get disqualified for injecting fresh runners, toward the end of each race. This would normally be done in the woodland, and it was difficult to identify it happening, but they did get caught. Sir Bob would usually finish each race in the top three, followed by Phil then myself in the top ten; we would have as many as five, and possibly more, in the top twelve. Each team had up to twelve runners, but only eight would count at the finish of each race. There would be up to 200 runners in each event.

There were other events, such as a Divisional Half Marathon League, and the events which took place in Berlin, such as the Berlin 25km and the Berlin Marathon – these were two high profile events. The Olympic Stadium in Berlin housed the HQ of the Berlin Brigade, and Stadium Barracks is where the HQ of BRIXMIS was located – a detachment that I would have loved to be a part of.

The 25km race would start just outside the Olympic Stadium, then weave a route around West Berlin. The event finished by entering a tunnel which went into the Olympic Stadium; you did a lap inside the tunnel, then entered the arena and completed one lap of the 400-metre track, finishing at the finish line. While running around the inside of the stadium, you could see the area where Adolf Hitler had once stood, in the 1936 Summer Olympics.

The Berlin Marathon started along Straße des 17. Juni, facing toward Victory Column. The Russian War Memorial was on the right-hand side, the Tiergarten to the left, with the Brandenburg Gate behind us. There would be thousands taking part, and once the gun had gone to start the race, it took quite some time for all the runners – who were queued on the grounds in front of the Reichstag – to loop around toward the start line. Victory Column was built between 1865 and 1873, to commemorate the Prussian Victory, though it once stood in front of the Reichstag; the Nazis dismantled it in 1938 and moved it to its current location, on the Großer Stern roundabout. After passing Victory Column, the route meandered its way through West Berlin, eventually following the route of the Berlin Wall past Potsdamer Platz, continuing along the wall, passing memorials for the people who had tried to escape from East Berlin but had been shot. When we passed Theodor-Heuss-Platz, we could see the flame in its big bowl atop a stone pillar. The flame itself would eventually be extinguished on Wednesday 3rd October 1990, the day of German unity, but was relit again on Monday 10th December 1990 (the "Day of Human Rights"), with the inscription *"Freiheit Recht Friede" ("Freedom, Right, Peace")*. The Berlin Marathon would eventually finish on the Kurfürstendamm, next to the Kaiser Wilhelm Gedächtnis-Kirche (Kaiser Wilhelm Memorial Church). It was and still is a very remarkable event, taking competitors on a historic journey through time, in one of the most beautiful cities in Europe.

Armed with all the knowledge and skills I had learnt from SMI Ordd, I went on my first instructor's course, at the Army School of Physical Training, the headquarters of the Royal Army Physical Training Corps (RAPTC).

The Army Gymnastics Staff were formed in 1860, after the Crimean War. In 1919 they were renamed the "Army Physical Training Staff", and by 1940 they had become the "Army Physical Training Corps". Her Majesty the Queen bestowed the title of "Royal" on the APTC in 2010.

The Corps, as they are often referred to, have three roles:

1. To maintain physical fitness throughout the Army.
2. Adventure training.
3. Rehabilitation of soldiers recovering from serious injuries and physiotherapy.

On day one of my course, we had to pass an entrance test. The whole course would be six weeks long, and all successful candidates would become Class 3 PTIs, able to plan and conduct trained soldiers in a wide range of physical activities and sports. The course embraces all the Army values, and demands enthusiasm, comradeship and team spirit; it pushed candidates to their physical limits, and each day we were inspected several times. We weren't worthy of wearing any of the kit associated with being a PTI until later in the course; until then we had to wear the black PT pumps, green socks rolled down, blue shorts and white or red PT vests, along with the tracksuits of our respective units, mine being 8 Regiment RCT.

I couldn't help reading one of the wall presentations at Fox Gym, about the qualities and definition of a sportsman. This definition was drawn up at a meeting in 1919, by representatives of the Army School of Physical Training, home forces, and British expeditionary forces from France, Italy, Egypt and Mesopotamia:

"A Sportsman:

1. *Plays the game for the game's sake;*
2. *Plays for his side and not for himself;*
3. *Is a good winner and a good loser, modest in victory and generous in defeat;*
4. *Accepts all decisions in a proper spirit;*
5. *Is chivalrous toward a defeated opponent;*
6. *Is unselfish and always ready to help others to become*

proficient;

7. *As a spectator applauds good play on both sides;*

8. *Never interferes with referees or judges, no matter what the decision."*

There were also classroom lessons in which we would study the function of the human body. These lessons were Anatomy and Physiology, and I found them fascinating; they not only gave us knowledge of all bodily systems, but they also provided knowledge about when things go wrong, and how to identify and treat common injuries in various sports.

It wasn't until our final tests and lesson observations that I bumped into who was now S/Sgt. Savage. At Taunton he was a PTI Class 2; now he was in the Corps. He recognized several of us and pulled us all to one side, stating: "Your lessons had best be good, and they *will* be good – after all, it was I that trained you."

On each day of week six we would be inspected. Now we all had a pair of itchy, navy-blue serge trousers, which had to be immaculately pressed, and a pair of white pumps. We each had red snake belts and white instructor vests, with the red crossed sabres in the middle of the chest. My vest was a bit baggy, but I was already like a rake, and having had six weeks of solid P.T. I had lost quite a bit of weight; in boxing terms I was a light-welterweight.

On one of the test days, we all presented ourselves to each of the RAPTC members, ready to raise our hands individually at each test station, and say: "Test Staff." Doc Savage was assessing the rope climbing, and I don't think anyone passed their first or second attempt. Climbing the rope wasn't a problem – there is a technique – but it was the bullshit involved. I presented myself to Doc Savage and said: "Test Staff."

He replied: "Rope climbing; you know what you have to do. If you want to take your vest off you may do so; it's up to you. There is a bench here for you to place your vest on."

I took off my vest and placed it on the bench. I didn't want any marks on it when I dismounted the rope; I wanted my vest to be clean for the next assessment.

"Mount the rope," Doc said.

My mount was perfect and I was breathing through my nose.

"And climb," he said

I reached the top of the rope and, after a perfect climb, I descended the rope. Having reached the bottom, I hovered just above the gym floor.

Doc said: "Dismount the rope."

I did so and it was perfect; I was still breathing through my nose. I waited for my feedback.

"Fail. You have two more attempts," Doc said.

I was gutted, but I continued with each of the other assessments. When I returned to the rope climbing, I said: "Test Staff."

Doc reminded me to place my vest on the bench if I so wished, and like before I placed my vest on the bench. Then he said: "Mount the rope."

I climbed the rope a second time then dismounted. Perfect.

I still failed. I was wracking my brain.

Then, on my third attempt, I folded my vest and placed it neatly next to him on the bench.

After dismounting, Doc said: "Pass. We expect the best from soldiers, so you must remember that your personal bullshit must be perfect – even if that means the smallest things, like folding up your vest, rather than just dropping it on the bench."

I had made lots more friends on the Class 3 PTI course, and on the day before we returned to our respective units, we were given our results. I had passed, but more importantly I had crossed a hurdle or a barrier. I had become an instructor in the British Army, and it was the first of many instructor courses that I would have the privilege of completing.

I had one week of leave before I returned to Münster. I went back to York and up into the Moors. It was while I was on this leave that I bumped into my friend from school, Steve.

I gave him a pat on the back and said: "How are you? You've had your hair cut." The same words he had said to me, after my basic training.

"Yep," Steve said, then: "get the beers in, Mark; you owe me that."

He had joined the Green Howards, and I was chuffed to bits with him. He wasn't at all cross with me, for showing him all that cash I had from Taunton and lying that one week's wages of a soldier were phenomenal; he just laughed now. Steve had already completed one operational tour of Northern Ireland, and was on his post-operational tour leave. He was stationed in Osnabrück, with the First Battalion, the Green Howards – "The Yorkshire Regiment" in Germany. It was only an hour-long bus or train ride from Münster.

Steve had done his basic training at Strensall, which was the HQ and depot of the King's Division, only a twenty-minute drive away from where he is from. He knew the instructors I had when I was at Taunton (Corporal Glennon and Corporal Ferguson). I was in my element. It suddenly struck me that the Army is a family, wherever you were born. It isn't just your biological parents who bring you up, but also the community you are exposed to: schools, Scouts and other youth organizations, your friends and even the people who run the corner shops. The Army is similar: there is always someone who either knows you directly, or they know you through someone else, and the qualities of those people brush off onto each other. When I thought of the values of the Army, and how those values bring people together, it all made sense.

When I returned to Münster I had done more growing up, but I was in for a shock: I was still a skinny rake, and my PTI vest still didn't fit.

QMSI Ordd did his usual Monday morning inspection of the PTIs, and when he got to me he laughed at my baggy PT vest. Then he congratulated me, smiled and said: "I think you've been a substantive Lance Corporal since you passed your course, but now you're the sprog PTI and you were voted in your absence to take CFTs for the rest of the week. Welcome back."

For the rest of that week I took troops from the RCT (27 Squadron and 13 Squadron), and platoons from the RPC (144 Company and 70 Company) on the Combat Fitness Test (CFT).

Each soldier's kit had to weigh 25kg, though some had different weights, depending on the role of that soldier, and whether they were in a combat, administrative or medical role. Added to the kit, each soldier carried their personal weapon. The CFT was an eight-mile TAB, which had to be completed within two hours. I did two eight-mile TABs a day, which had to be timed. Instructors were then required to demonstrate the technique of a fireman's lift, so that the troops could safely complete a 100-metre carry. In addition to all that, I had to mop up the individuals like chefs, stores personnel and clerks, who needed to complete their tests.

Over the next year or so, I continued working in the gym, taking remedial P.T. sessions, circuit training and taking part in various sport activities. I had made a lot of friends, not just in the Pioneers but also in the RCT, the RA, RAPC and even one or two in the RMP.

I was due to go on two weeks leave, but before I went I needed to take one P.T. lesson, which was to be a mop-up CFT. It turned out that this would be my last eight-mile TAB for a few months. This CFT was going to be a good one; nothing could go wrong.

I got up, made my bed and tidied up my room. I was dressed in combat trousers with my red snake belt, boots and putties, and my new PTI tracksuit top, with crossed sabres above the Lance Corporal chevron. I went to the cookhouse and had some breakfast, then went across to the gym. Once in the gym I made the CQMS a coffee and waited until my group of mixed cap badges came along for registering. There were two lads who were training to go on their PTI courses, and they were to accompany me as my traffic markers, one at the front and one to the rear. I briefed both markers about the route, then went to get the scales out of the gym store, ready to weigh the kit of the soldiers.

My group arrived on time at 10:30 sharp. They had their personal weapons, which were all SLRs. If ever we took lessons which involved weapon systems, we would always carry out N.S.P.s (normal safety precautions), and once all weapons had been cleared and I had reminded my markers about traffic, I turned the squad in the direction we were going in.

I shouted: "BY THE FRONT... QUICK MARCH!" Then I started the stopwatch.

The CFT route took us along the Ems Canal toward Gremmendorf, on the opposite side of Münster. My markers would stop traffic as we crossed each road, then halfway we would get the troops to drink from their water bottles. The test was going very well, and we eventually returned to Portsmouth Barracks.

As we got through the main gate, I broke the squad into quick time, then wheeled them round to the parade square, to do the fireman's carry and climb into a truck part of the test. I got one of my markers and asked him to adopt a position, making it easier to demonstrate how to lift someone. Then, as I picked up the marker, I felt a rip in my lower abdomen. I thought nothing of it and we continued with the test. As I demonstrated how to climb into a truck, this time I felt a very sharp pain where I had felt the rip.

I stood up and conducted that part of the test, cleared all the weapons again and dismissed the group, who had all passed. Then I took the register into the gym so that it could be processed and Part Two Ordered; this is where the names of the group being tested would be published as proof of passing their CFT or BFT. I took the completed paperwork to the Regimental HQ, which was only up a small flight of stairs.

I took the first and second step, then I felt another rip. I was okay then, but by the third step I couldn't stand up straight – and I needed to, because RSM Dave Jurgens was on his way down the steps, and I needed to brace up in a mark of respect. He was a total gentleman in the RCT, and was very well-liked and respected by the whole regiment and the British Army. Then my body just buckled, with a stabbing pain in my lower abdomen.

All I could hear was the RSM shouting: "It wasn't me! I didn't touch him!" as the Adjutant followed him through the swing doors. Both the RSM and the Adjutant sat me down on a step.

The Adjutant said: "Are you okay, Corporal Nichol?"

I replied: "I don't know, sir... I felt a rip. But I need to take this paperwork to the orderly room." I tried to stand up, but my body wasn't having it.

I undid my belt and trousers, and even doing that I could feel that something wasn't quite right. I had a huge lump, which had formed just above my pubes on the left-hand side; it stretched towards my left hip. I apologized to the RSM.

"Don't be daft, young Mark!" he said. "Yer hurting, lad." He was concerned and wanted to help.

A couple of medics were summoned; one of them was Mick.

"What ya done, Mark?" asked Mick.

I replied: "I dunno."

"Pull yer trousers down; lets 'av' a look."

The lump was now about the same size as my fist and was starting to bruise.

Mick said: "We need to get you to BMH (British Military Hospital) now; you have a strangulated hernia. You will probably need an operation." I had never had an operation before.

Mick the medic and his RAMC (Royal Army Medical Corps) colleague managed to get me to the medical centre of 8 Regiment. I didn't feel much in terms of pain, but there was some discomfort. I was transported immediately to BMH Münster and taken to a ward.

I know that all hospitals are spotless, but this was gleaming. I had been in hospitals before, to visit friends and family, and there was always a clinical smell, but this hospital smelled more like a barracks block after a bull night, in preparation for a CO and RSM's block inspection. Prior to 1945, BMH Münster had been a Wehrmacht H.Q.; the military part of the building was housed in one wing of the German krankenhaus (hospital).

I was very well looked after, and operated on the following morning; I consider myself to be lucky. Someone told me that there are two sorts of friends: the fair-weather friends, who might say hello and have the odd pint with you if they need something, and then the proper friends, who come and visit you in hospital. I had dozens of visits, and word had got out, so I had friends visiting from Duisburg, Bielefeld, and even Steve my old schoolmate came by.

Steve said: "I'm on the lash tonight, Mark. I've moved into your room and I'm occupying your bedspace. Only for this weekend, though, then I'm on leave for two weeks. I knew you wouldn't mind." There was a chance that Steve and I could be on the same coach home on leave, because I would get a one-week sick leave.

By my third afternoon in BMH, my CSM, the CO, the RSM and QMSI had visited. Steve and the rest of my visitors all had something in common

– the same something that RSMs and CSMs all have: they all cared.

"The simple act of caring is heroic."

Edward Albert.

I was in BMH for one week, after which I went on sick leave with my new scar. I was given very strict instructions from the Matron when I left BMH Münster. She was a Colonel in the Queen Alexander Royal Army Nursing Corps (QARANC), who reminded me of Mrs. Allot, my very first teacher from school.

"You're going on leave now, Corporal Nichol."

"Yes, Ma'am."

Then she said: "If I discover that you have done any PT or training while you're on leave you will face disciplinary action – just be aware of that, Corporal Nichol."

"Yes, Ma'am."

"You need to report back here in seven days for your stitches to be taken out, then you will go back on leave for two more weeks, I'm afraid; this envelope has your travel warrants. Enjoy your leave."

I wasn't going to question why I needed to come back to Münster, but it seemed a bit of a waste to be going on leave to York for a week, return to Münster for a day, then back to York the following day; surely stitches could have been taken out in York? But, there is a strict protocol within the military, and it was only the doctor in Münster who could release me from their care, after I had been checked over and given a clean and fit bill of health. I wasn't going to protest; I daren't.

I asked the duty driver to take me to Gremmendorf to catch the Transline coach, which would leave Gremmendorf NAAFI each Friday at 17:00. It would take passengers all the way to Waterloo and King's Cross train stations in London, arriving at King's Cross at about 07:30 the following morning.

As I boarded the coach and showed my ticket, I heard a voice say: "Marky, come and sit here." It was Steve, my old schoolfriend from the Green Howards; he had boarded the coach in Osnabrück.

London is a huge European city and the capital of the UK; I didn't have a clue about finding my way around. Unlike Berlin, which would eventually become the capital of Germany; I knew Berlin very well. Our coach was only half full when it dropped a handful of passengers at Waterloo, then the rest of us at King's Cross.

Because Steve and I couldn't exchange our warrants until later that day, our departure from London wasn't until late that afternoon, so we would arrive at York later that evening; we had the whole day to wander around London. We even practiced travelling on the tube.

After something to eat, we managed to find our way to Oxford Street. It reminded me of the Ku'damm in Berlin, a very busy shopping area, even at half-past ten in the morning. Steve suggested that we should find a pub to sit in and have a beer. A lot of the pubs we visited in London had the usual lager you might expect to find in any pub in the UK, but we were both interested in the bitter, and I must admit our first pint was quite nice; the head clung to the inside of the glass, all the way until the glass was empty. The barman of the first pub recommended a very dark beer which had a sweet taste, called London Pride; it was delicious. After we had drunk two pints, we went to visit a pub on a corner, which had been recommended by the barman; the second pub was only a short walk away. They had London Pride and some other stuff, but it wasn't quite as nice. Steve and I visited three other pubs, and had a whale of a time before returning to King's Cross, where we exchanged our travel warrants and made our way to the platform.

Once on the train, the journey would only take a couple of hours. I just needed to look out for the platform signs reading *"York"*, then we would leave the train. Just one job... and I couldn't even do that right! Steve and I fell asleep, completely missed York and ended up in Darlington.

It was now close to 20:30, and we couldn't get back to York for a couple of hours. Then I had an idea: we could catch the Malton bus from Darlington. I knew there was a bus which travelled down Blakey Ridge and I was gambling on the Malton bus; maybe if I asked the bus driver nicely, he could stop for us at the Lion Inn on Blakey Ridge. The whole idea was daft, but we chose that option, and it did turn out to be in our favour; we only had to wait for fifteen minutes. We asked the bus driver if he drove that route, and if he wouldn't mind dropping us off. The bus was quite a posh one, but we were able to pay £3.75 each for the journey.

The bus stopped at Danby, then continued to Hutton le Hole, then on to Pickering and Malton. The driver did drop us off at the Lion Inn, which had been my final delivery on my old weekend paper round. What a journey; it was now half-past nine. The Lion Inn was open and serving, so we sat at the bar, and had several more beers and something to eat.

Steve and I had lost track of time, and when I looked at my watch it was past midnight. Though only a few miles away, I wasn't going to enjoy waking my grandparents up for a lift. The landlord was called Harry, the same landlord who had been at the Lion Inn when I did my paper round, and he agreed with me.

Harry had a stammer, and would often stutter when talking to people. It was important not to help him to speak, by predicting and saying on his behalf the words Harry was struggling with; he would struggle to speak if he was stressed. Grace, one of local girls from Rosedale, sang in a choir, and very often she would encourage Harry to sing his words, rather than speaking them, so Harry did often sing what he was trying to say. What I found amazing was that Harry did have a very good voice when he sang. He would go on to become a choir member.

"Ooh, ooh, n-no, d-d-don't go wecking Victor up, y-yer g-g-grandad," Harry went on to say; "aah shall gi' thi't lift."

Instead of accepting, I asked to borrow a torch; the weather was good, so we could walk. We left the Lion Inn at close to 02:00, taking a shortcut across the moor at the back of the Lion Inn, toward the old disused railway that I used to cycle along; there was a path down into Farndale, along the edge of a wood. There was a tiny bit of drizzle, but we found our way, with the torch Harry the landlord had kindly loaned us; Grandad could return it to Harry a day or so later. This worked out well for Grandad and Harry: Grandad now had a licence from Gran to visit the Lion Inn and have several beers with Harry... but Gran would have to drive.

It was close to 03:00 when we weaved our way down the dale, and came across that old cowhouse we kipped in only a few years previous, when I was fourteen years old. I didn't want to wake up my grandparents, so Steve said: "Let's get our heads down in here, Mark." It was warm enough, the light still worked and there were plenty of bales of straw.

Moments later, Tinker the old yard cat strolled in. He was a kitten when I had first met him, and he was a good mouser. He had no permanent home, but locals would leave saucers of milk and food out for all the yard cats, to keep the rat and mouse populations down – and the moggies were good at it. Tinker strolled in with his tail up in the air, purring. He curled up next to Steve and looked up at us. If Tinker could have spoken, I am sure he would have said: "Just like old times."

Chapter 8
Heidi and Jason

"Our dreams can come true if we have the courage to pursue them."

Walt Disney.

"There are no constraints on the human mind, no walls around the human spirit, no barriers to our progress, except those that we ourselves erect."

Ronald Reagan.

I didn't really know Jason or Heidi, but I knew of them; then, eventually I would be involved in a mission with them, somewhere along the IGB (Inner German Border) and Berlin. Jason was in 5 Squadron RCT; he was a Corporal, and during exercises he was the 5 Squadron OC's driver. I would often see Jason around the barracks, and I even took him on a CFT (combat fitness test) and a BFT (basic fitness test). Heidi would often be in the 5 Squadron bar or in the Corporals' Mess with Jason. They would both say hello.

Having discovered that I was from Yorkshire, Heidi would often try to speak with a Yorkshire accent. She once commented that I spoke good, acceptable German, but with a Yorkshire accent – which to me was a compliment.

Heidi was tall, with blonde hair and dark eyes, and her story was amazing. She had been born in Berlin in 1958; she lived in East Berlin before the wall was built. Both her parents worked: her father was a train driver for the Deutsche Reichsbahn, or DR, which was the operating name of state-owned railways in the German Democratic Republic (East Germany). Heidi's mother also worked, in the forests around Amt Oberspreewald, near Drachhausen, which is about 100 km from where their family home was. Both parents worked hard, and would very often be working shifts.

On the night of 12th August 1961, construction of the Berlin Wall began. Heidi would have been three years old at the time and she was with her grandparents (Oma and Opa) who lived in Wilmersdorf (West Berlin); Heidi wasn't due to see her mother and father until the following Tuesday. But Heidi wouldn't hug or embrace her parents for decades, until the Cold War began to thaw in 1989; their whole family had been torn apart by the construction of the wall. The only way Heidi could see her parents was by standing on one of the viewing platforms which had been constructed along the inside or Western sector of the wall, and hoping that she might catch a glimpse of them across in East Berlin. No one had home telephones in those days; they were a luxury reserved only for the government officials in East Germany. From time to time, Heidi would write letters to her parents, but she would only receive two or three letters back each year. Phone calls and mail were intercepted by Stasi, and Eastern Bloc citizens would often be targeted if they were communicating with people from the West.

At the age of ten, Heidi moved with her grandparents to Hanover, where she continued to go to school. By the age of sixteen she was a very fluent speaker of English and French; she must have been a star student at school. She would eventually be employed as an interpreter for West German government offices in Münster, Osnabrück and Bielefeld.

In 1986, Jason and Heidi decided that they wanted to get married; Heidi was twenty-seven years old. Germans traditionally got married at a government civil registry office, then after the ceremony they would often wish to attend a church service, for a wedding blessing. When Jason mentioned that they were going to get married, I said:

"Have you been to see the Padre? He can work miracles."

"I might just do that," Jason said,

About a week passed, then I saw Jason again. He told me: "I think the Padre might want to see you."

Then he asked me: "Do you know your way around Berlin, or any parts of the IGB?"

"Yes, I do," I said; "I know both quite well." I went on to say that I had done countless IGB patrols, all the way from just south of Helmeted, to Salzwedel, on to Horst then all the way up to Lübeck. I informed Jason that I had a very good set of maps, which were the latest editions, extending into parts of East Germany, close to the Iron Curtain.

Jason said: "Good; I think the Padre may want to chat to you, then."

Later, the QMSI shouted into the gym: "Mark… phone; it's Major Milne."

I ran back to the gym office and picked up the phone; "Lance Corporal Nichol, sir."

It was my OC (Officer Commanding), requesting my presence at once.

"I will be there straight away, sir," I said.

The OC was Major Ian Milne, a former Royal Marines Commando. He was a Scot and had a mild accent. He had sent me on LRRPG (Long Range Reconnaissance Patrol Group) school, and I would often accompany him on tasks to speak German. He displayed qualities similar to those of the CO Colonel Barlet, and like Colonel Barlet, Major Milne knew everyone's first name in the regiment. When I arrived at his office, I braced up.

"Ah, Mark," he said, "in you come, lad. Relax and sit down."

He sat down behind his desk and dialled a number, waited then said: "Hello, Andy, it's Ian. I have Mark here; can I send him over? Righto, I'll send him over." He put down the phone and said to me: "Right then, Mark, you are going on a task with the Padre, and possibly the OC of 5 Squadron. Go and see the Padre; he is expecting you. You and a section are going to Berlin; you're going to visit several villages close to the Elbe River, to identify somewhere along the IGB suitable for a wedding venue and blessing."

"I think I know who that might be for," I said. "Thank you, sir."

"Don't worry about it," he said, "but that's a beer you owe me."

The Padre was waiting in his office.

"In you come, Mark. Sit down."

The Padre explained that he needed to go to Berlin for three meetings, and that I was going with him. We would be there for one week and would be staying at Edinburgh House, a hotel on Theodor-Heuss-Platz, used by British servicemen and women, and their families.

Theodor-Heuss-Platz is a square, with gardens and pathways running through the middle, and roads surrounding the whole square. The square itself was laid out as part of the development of the new West End district of Berlin, between 1904 and 1908, and named Reichskanzlerplatz, after the office of the Imperial Chancellor. Then, on 21st April 1933, after the Nazi seizure of power, the square was renamed Adolf-Hitler-Platz. After World War II, on 31st July 1947, the square was renamed again, officially returned to its original name of Reichskanzlerplatz. It wasn't until six days after the death of President Theodor Heuss, on 18th December 1963, that the square was given its present name, Theodor-Heuss-Platz.

This would be my second visit to Edinburgh House. It was lovely. Even the OC of 5 Squadron laughed and said: "A bit posh for you, isn't it,

Mark?"

I would have my own room, there were waitresses and waiters, wine and beer, and to top it all we would be travelling on the Berliner train. All I needed to pack was my barrack dress, with a number 2 shirt and a tie, one set of lightweight trousers, a jersey heavy wool, a pair of boots, PTI kit and snake belt, a pair of issued shoes and beret.

On the day of our departure, we were taken by car to Hanover, to board the train. The OC of 5 Squadron, the Padre and I all wore casual civvies with nice shoes. As we approached Braunschweig, I pointed out to the Padre and the OC a location we used on IGB patrols, to the left and right of the train. On our approach to Helmeted, I also pointed out other places of interest. Across the border, we could see the Eastern Bloc troops patrolling, observing us through high-powered lenses.

I was fascinated by the IGB. Try to think of an old medieval castle; you might have visited one or two of the many in the British Isles. Motte and bailey structure castles were built post-1066, whilst stone-built castles had their advantages and disadvantages, in much the same way that the Iron Curtain had its pros and cons. Old wooden castles could easily be set on fire or rot, but they had a motte, which was a good advantage. The Iron Curtain didn't have a motte, but it did have deep ditches with a ramp, meaning it would be difficult for vehicles from the West to get across, because of the steep-sided ditch; however, invading forces from the East would have crossed the ditches with ease, because of the ramp which they could drive up. The Iron Curtain did not have steep, high, curved castle walls; instead, it had a twelve- to fifteen-feet wall all the way along, with a cylindrical structure on the top, to prevent people with grappling hooks tied to a rope from climbing over; the same as the Berlin Wall. Medieval castles only had one entry/exit point, which was a weak point, whereas the IGB only had very few crossing points, such as the roads and railways, which were very heavily guarded. Other roads that did exist prior to 1947 had been dug up, so you could drive along a minor road toward the IGB, then, as you approached the Iron Curtain, the road would come to an end, continuing on the other side of no man's land; the bit of road in-between no longer existed. There was no portcullis on each entry point; the roads just had barriers painted red and white, or black and yellow. The IGB had concrete watchtowers instead of crenellations, and each watchtower had a small opening, to afford a good firing point. The windows were armoured glass, to prevent penetration of small-arms fire. There were no sharp pikes that medieval castles had; instead, there were tank traps and vehicle traps. In a way, the Iron Curtain resembled Hadrian's Wall or the Great Wall of China – just a more up to date version.

Just over the border, the train came to a halt at Marienborn and changed engines. There was the usual parade which was always done on the platform, followed by Soviet officials boarding the train to check our NATO travel orders and identity cards.

As the train pulled out of Marienborn, the Padre asked what my local knowledge of the IGB was like. I told him that I knew my way around the West side of the border, and that I had done plenty of patrols; all the maps that I had were marked and up to date.

Then he said: "Are there any nice picture postcard areas of no man's land?"

I was beginning to think that the Padre was going to try rescuing someone from the East, and help them escape to the West. I replied: "I can think of a few in woodland, where you can see over the border into the East." I mentioned also that there were two small villages in the DDR, tight against the border, which both had churches. I explained that the Iron Curtain and no man's land was a strip of land about 1,400 kilometres long, which ran from the Baltic Sea to Czechoslovakia. The strip of land varied in width from about one hundred metres to about a kilometre. I continued to say that there were signs which bore the words, *"Halt. Hier Grenze. Bundesgrenzschutz"*, meaning *"Stop. Here is the Border. Federal Boundary Guard"*. From one of these signs, you could see all the different zones of the Iron Curtain.

From the West side there were the border signs, then a huge fence, which extended underground to a depth of four metres. It was often referred to as the "rabbit fence" and was designed to prevent would-be escapees from absconding to the West. Then there was a bit of wasteland, a ditch then another fence, beyond which was the "Death Strip" which was littered with mines and booby-traps. This part of the strip was sandy and much of the ordnance there was visible; you could see where a lot of the mines were. Some anti-personnel mines were also attached to the fences.

There was additionally what appeared to be a long strip of sand, which was inspected and raked by Soviet and East German forces, to identify footsteps of would-be escapees. Behind that was a road lit by streetlamps, and regularly patrolled by Soviet and East German forces. There were also low, single-wire fences, which looked almost like washing lines, with a chain about ten metres long; at one end of the chain there was a ring attached to the washing line, and at the other end was a guard dog – these were at intervals along no man's land.

Toward the other side were watchtowers, with huge searchlights, machine-gun posts and observation towers. There was another rabbit fence, which had sensors to alert troops in watchtowers and an electric fence, followed by a controlled zone, from which locals would be moved on by the East German police.

The whole thing was a maze of vehicle and tank traps, booby-traps and other nasty barriers, to prevent Western influence on East German citizens. The vehicle traps were made from five- to ten-feet lengths of girder or railway line, which were cemented into the ground then welded together halfway up. They were often called "hedgehogs"; tanks and other vehicles could not cross them.

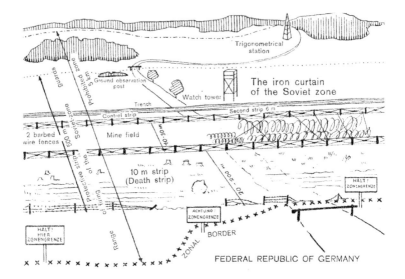

Where the train crossed the border, the width of no man's land would have been about one hundred metres. The Padre asked if there were any other, narrower parts of the strip. There were other parts of no man's land which weren't very wide, due to the geographical lay of the ground, with rivers here and there flowing parallel to the border.

When we arrived in Charlottenburg, transport was waiting to take us to Edinburgh House, to drop off the OC and Padre, then Stadium Barracks, where I was to be accommodated; I had my own room in transit accommodation.

Later that afternoon, I met the Padre and the OC at their hotel bar in Edinburgh House; they permitted me to join them for an evening meal. I had to display good manners and drink red wine, which was unusual for me; I am more of a beer lover. The OC was due to have a meeting at HQ Berlin Brigade the following morning, while the Padre had to attend a meeting at the Blue Church; I was still not sure what my involvement would be.

The Kurfürstendamm, or Ku'damm, is always bursting with life, and is a main shopping area of West Berlin. At the East end of the Ku'damm is the Kaiser Wilhelm Memorial Church, often called Gedächtniskirche – the British call it the "Blue Church"; it is usually where the Berlin Marathon would finish. The Blue Church was built by Franz Schwechten, between 1891 and 1895, and comprises the ruins of the church which was destroyed in the war, as well as a modern church building. The church is a memorial for peace and reconciliation, and commemorates Berliners' determination to rebuild after WW2. It is a place of contemplation; once you leave the maddening crowds and enter the Blue Church, it is total silence inside. Most of the glass tiles are blue, giving the church its appearance.

The Padre told me: "I have a meeting at the Blue Church in the morning, then I must be at Stadium Barracks at 13:30. I need you to go to Stadium Barracks and find BRIXMIS Headquarters, to talk to someone about this letter I have here. The visit will be in your interest." He handed me the envelope. "Now, how would I get to the Blue Church, Mark?"

"Come on, Your Holiness," I said, "let me introduce you to the Ku'damm and I'll take you to the Kaiser Wilhelm Church; we might even stop on the way so that I can introduce you to German beer – not that wine stuff you drink, but proper German beer in its purest form."

While out walking along the Ku'damm the Padre announced that the Soviets were currently guarding Spandau prison; the Soviet, British, French and American forces usually took it in turns on PGF (Prison Guard Force) duties. The Soviets had two footholds in West Berlin: the Soviet War Memorial and prison guard duties at Spandau prison. The building of

Spandau prison was completed in 1881, and it only housed a handful of Nazi war criminals, convicted at the Nuremberg trials, the last, sole inmate being Rudolf Hess. Hess died in 1987, after a suspected suicide, aged 93.

Next to the prison was Smuts Barracks, which was built between 1883 and 1886, and had been a train and railways unit. It was ideal for tank units because of the railhead to transport tanks, and during WW2 it housed an S.S. panzer division.

In an attempt to create disruption in West Berlin, the Soviet forces would deliberately push our forces to call Active Edge. This would often happen when the Soviets were guarding Spandau prison. There were a few scaffolding frames, which could be used to erect towers between the main watchtowers, and this would normally be done in foggy conditions. If an observer in one of the main towers couldn't see the next tower because of fog or mist, the scaffolds could be quickly erected halfway between each tower, so that observers could see each other, and were easily able to observe over the wall, into Smuts Barracks.

It was late summer and the weather was lovely: a sunny day with no fog. But the Soviets had erected two towers along the back wall of the prison, to look over into Smuts Barracks. Active Edge would be called in Berlin if the Soviets were doing exercises close to the borders, or if there was Soviet troop movement and extra tanks been moved toward Berlin; BRIXMIS would usually be able to notify HQ Berlin of any troop movement. Once Active Edge had been called by the British, the Soviets would time and record how long it took for the British troops in Smuts Barracks to be mobilized. The tanks would deploy to positions in the Mite (central) area of Berlin, and around the Tiergarten. You could tell when MBTs (main battle tanks) had been deployed, because the roads and pavements would have been churned up by tank tracks; this would cost the West millions of dollars in road repairs every year.

I would catch up with the OC the next day; I was to accompany the OC while the Padre attended his meeting at the Blue Church. My dress code was barrack dress, but wearing shirt sleeve order (shirt sleeves rolled up); even though it was sunny, there was a chill in the air. The OC knew his way to Stadium Barracks and he arrived shortly after 09:00. I met him close to the Olympic Stadium, only a short walk across the huge, paved forecourt of the stadium, from where the Berlin 25km race starts. Once in the stadium, the OC knew where we were going.

BRIXMIS had offices along a corridor and part of an underground complex, where vehicles were serviced and garaged. The OC of the Mission was over the bridge, in the Potsdam Mission House; to get to the Mission House, BRIXMIS would drive their vehicles over the Glienicke Bridge, which is where the Eastern Bloc and the West would exchange spies, political prisoners and other persons of interest. I had only ever seen the bridge during the winter, covered in snow; at the far end, you could see the East German forces. The Soviet forces didn't really go to the bridge, but if they did it was usually to exchange people. Each visit to the bridge I had been on always brought a strange atmosphere or mood to the day – this was as far forward any battle line could have been drawn. The bridge itself crossed the Havel River, and was the only access for diplomats and military missions; Checkpoint Charlie was only used by civilians.

The bridge had originally been constructed of wood, to allow access for the population of Berlin to hunting ground. But it was badly damaged by bombing in WW2, and needed to be rebuilt; the reconstruction of the steel bridge was not completed until 1949. The East German government named it the "Bridge of Unity", as the border between East Germany and Western Allies-occupied West Berlin ran across the middle of the bridge. By the 1970s, the bridge had outlived its projected lifespan and needed significant repairs; the cost of these repairs became a focus of dispute between the government of West Berlin and the government of East Germany. In 1980, the West Berlin government repaired its half of the bridge, and in 1985 the West Berlin government paid for repairs to the East German half of the bridge, in exchange for formally renaming the bridge "Glienicke Bridge", from "Bridge of Unity". On the evening of 10th November 1989, one day after the opening of the Berlin Wall, the Glienicke Bridge was reopened for pedestrians. Border fortifications and barricades were dismantled, as part of German reunification in 1990.

BRIXMIS had both Army and RAF attached to them. When we arrived, there was an RAF Flight Sergeant Colin Williamson there, whom I recognized from my LRRP course. He introduced me to his boss, a Squadron Leader:

"This is Corporal Andrew Nichol, boss."

I shook both hands and introduced the OC. The OC was expected at a briefing, and I was free now. The OC said: "See you in about two hours, Corporal Nichol." Then he went for his meeting.

I said to Colin: "I hope that the Padre is okay. He has a meeting at the Blue Church, then he needs to be here at 13:30."

"I know," Colin said. "We'll go and pick him up; we can set off once we return from RAF Gatow. Come on, let's go for a drive."

Somehow, I knew that BRIXMIS would know the whereabouts of everyone, even our Padre. Yet I felt totally relaxed and at home in the BRIXMIS offices; I knew exactly what their role was: they were nicknamed "Cold War Spies".

Down in the garage area, we climbed into a top of the range BRIXMIS Mercedes Gelaendewagen. We drove for a while toward RAF Gatow, where Colin had to pick up a clerk, two all-singing-all-dancing cameras and five boxes of 35mm film; they would use these to take photos of the East Germans and the Soviet land and air forces, across in the East.

I was hooked on wanting to be attached to BRIXMIS, even if only for a month or so. Lots of soldiers my age wanted to attempt SAS selection, the Para course and Commando course, but I had done LRRP School and could speak German quite fluently, with some knowledge of East German dialects. BRIXMIS was literally a mission for a person with other qualities and skills; it would take NATO troops right into the belly of the beast.

"Is this role something you would consider, Mark?" Colin asked.

"Ooh, Colin, now let me think about that… hmm, I've thought about it: of course I would!"

"The Padre might be able to pull a few strings," he said.

Colin now had my full attention, and I couldn't wait to get to a phone, to seek permission from the OC and CO back in Münster.

Colin asked: "Do you have any other uniform, Mark?"

I explained that I only had what I was wearing, one set of combats, PT kit and a jersey heavy wool, back at Stadium Barracks.

"Good, that's a start," said Colin.

Back at Stadium Barracks, I saw the OC of 5 Squadron and walked over toward him. Before I even opened my mouth to speak, he said:

"The answer to your next question is a provisional yes – providing your OC and the CO approve."

"How did you know I was going to ask for six months leave, sir?" I laughed. "Only joking, sir. But it would be a fantastic opportunity to join BRIXMIS on a detachment prior to being posted; I would be the only Chunky (Royal Pioneer) ever to be attached to them." The OC of 5 Squadron had been an officer for BRIXMIS, as had the 2IC of 144 Company.

There was a movements officer within the RCT, and he mentioned that there were five personnel from the unit entitled to some leave, so there was an opportunity for me to be temporarily attached to BRIXMIS, to cover while they were away. He said: "I will be phoning the CO this afternoon, then he will contact me here tomorrow, once he has spoken to Major Milne; they should be able to Part Two Order, promoting you to a local Corporal, or even an acting full Corporal – then at least you would be paid that rank."

I was totally over the moon. Something told me that I was going to be at BRIXMIS for several months.

All BRIXMIS personnel had to attend a briefing. There wasn't just Army and RAF; lots of civilian staff also provided support. In all, there must have been close to a hundred people who made up BRIXMIS. I needed to attend. The briefing was given by a civilian member of staff called Karl. Karl had long, dark hair and a moustache, was of average build but quite tall. He spoke fluently in English and Russian.

There were two civilian support staff, Felix and Mila, who also attended the briefing. I think they were of the opinion that the briefing should be done in English, seeing as there was now an Englishman there; when I introduced myself in German, I think it came as a bit of a relief, and the briefing was conducted in German. There were a few words that I got stuck on, but my new friends helped me. Felix was 27 years old, also with long hair, about five-and-a-half-feet tall. Mila was 34 years old, with short, blonde hair. Mila later explained how the wall divided her family, with the East German secret police, the Stasi, holding part of her family under duress.

The briefing informed us all about the terms of the Robert Malinin Agreement, which mentioned *"Building immune administration by the occupying forces"*, meaning that SOXMIS, BRIXMIS, the French Mission (FMLM) and US missions (USMLM) missions would all be treated respectfully; occupying forces would not treat opposing forces with violence, or deliberately damage property – like, for example, vehicles, which would very often need to be recovered by a "recce mech" (recovery mechanic) from the REME, as a result of being rammed or forced off the road by Soviet forces. The briefing explained the Stasi and Soviet view of BRIXMIS, stating: *"The mission (BRIXMIS) must comply with the rules and not violate prohibited areas. However, it has a job of observation, and can do it tactically, tactfully and with good manners, and still be observing the rules."*

Liaison briefings between Soviet and British senior officers were sometimes held at the Mission House in Potsdam, normally in comfort, in the form of a dinner, while day to day liaisons were held in Potsdam with the Soviet External Relations Bureau (SERB). BRIXMIS had tours out on the ground, every day of each year of its 44-year existence.

Eventually, the OC of BRIXMIS and the Padre told me what the contents of the letter were: details of where a wedding blessing ceremony would take place. This letter was to be delivered to the parents of Heidi. There was no address on the envelope and it couldn't be posted, because it would be intercepted and possibly never reach Heidi's mum and dad. People were allowed to travel from the East to the West to attend weddings, but this was never going to happen in this case, because the marriage was to a British soldier.

The following day, the OC of the BRIXMIS Mission arrived, as I had just made some of the staff in the BRIXMIS offices a brew. The OC was from the Royal Tank Regiment, and was accompanied by a Captain from the Army Intelligence Corps, who looked at me, then shook my hand and said:

"Welcome aboard, Mark."

This was followed by the OC saying: "Come into my office, Mark. Ooh, and bring a coffee – NATO standard, please."

The Padre and OC of 5 Squadron gave me the thumbs up.

I had to take my jumper and a combat jacket to the tailors, to have my

L/Cpl. chevron replaced with two chevrons, and new BRIXMIS patches sewn on. I was also required to do a big favour for my new temporary OC: he knew I was a PTI, so I had to take him and some of the Army staff on a BFT around the stadium… and no one failed.

Permission was granted for four months, which would see me through Christmas and into February of 1987. I would be required to fill in for people while they were on privileged leave and Christmas leave.

I had become more familiar with West Berlin, but now I was going to be in the East, developing my local knowledge of the eastern side of the Iron Curtain – though more so to identify where I would deliver the letter the Padre had. The contents – an invitation to the wedding blessing – were to be handed over by hand, directly to Heidi's parents; I would soon find myself meeting her mum and dad. By December of 1986, BFPO (British Forces Post Office) had posted a letter to HQ Berlin from Jason, identifying the location of the wedding blessing. Soon after, the Mission Commander sanctioned a recce to the village of Cumlosen which is on the north side of the Elbe River, right on the border of East and West Germany. From Cumlosen you could clearly see the West, and the village of Schnackenburg.

The width of no man's land was just over 100 metres, but surprisingly it was hardly patrolled by Soviet or East German forces, due to the river. There was a forest on the West side of the curtain, and on one night when I visited, I could hear people talking in the West. This was going to be an ideal post for Heidi's parents to attend the marriage of Heidi and Jason. BFPO were somehow also able to identify the house where Heidi's parents lived, in Jännersdorf; it was the Padre that was able to get this information, when he had visited the Blue Church; we were able to research the village of Jännersdorf and the home of Heidi's mum and dad.

On Friday 16th January 1987, I was sat in the back seat of an Opel

Senator 3.0i. My mission was to visit the village of Jännersdorf and deliver by hand the letter the Padre had been given; it was in a plain envelope, with no writing or markings to compromise my mission. I was wearing a pair of wellingtons, blue trousers, a green pullover and overalls; I had an East German army overcoat and the letter was in my pocket. There were no East German police or Soviet forces; the training areas weren't where we were going. It was a very clear night, with hardly any wind, and smoke from chimneys was going straight up. There was almost a full moon, which was bright enough to cast shadows and give the landscape a blueish colour. Some snow here and there, but mostly frost, which crackled underfoot. At 18:45 I was dropped off close to a road junction, about three hundred metres away from the village of Jännersdorf. I had no maps, just in case I was compromised; I had to remember the family name and address. I would be picked up close to a small chapel on the other side of the village, at exactly 19:45.

I had previously looked at a map and an aerial photograph, made a comparison, then memorized as best I could. On the aerial photograph there appeared to be a wall, with bushes dotted along it, which came to a sharp point to the north of a graveyard. The photograph would have been taken at roughly midday and the weather would have been clear, with the sun casting shadows of tall structures, which could be seen toward the north. There was no foliage on the bushes or trees, indicating that the photo would have been taken in the winter months. A power station's cooling towers were blowing steam west from an easterly wind, indicating that when the photo was taken it would have been cold weather conditions, just like now. There was some ice and snow.

I waited for several minutes. There was no traffic, so I walked past what looked like a bus stop, toward a rough track. The track had trees on either side, and followed the direction I ideally needed to walk in. At the edge of Jännersdorf, I could see a play area forming part of a village park, with flowerbeds which would soon be filled with springtime flowers, like daffodils; the park had swings, a slide and frames for kids to climb on. The whole place looked deserted; the only clue that anyone lived here were the lights I could see in windows. In a way, I felt lonely; it reminded me of the Iron Maiden track, "Stranger in a Strange Land", from the *Somewhere in Time* album released the previous September. I was a stranger in a strange land. I wasn't lost, but I was far from home, and there was no safety rope for me; I was on my own.

I saw a three-storey apartment block and a small Deutsche Post, the East German, state-operated post office. I only had a short distance to go, when I saw some people enter what looked like a bar. When I reached the bar, I could see through the window Radeberger (an East German beer) signs, and people playing the dice game "Shock Out". Within minutes, I had reached my objective.

I walked through a small gate and knocked on a door. I could hear movement inside, but could see only a small light. Then the door was opened by a young man, who would be about the same age I was. I asked if he was Herr Möller.

He nodded and asked me in, out of the cold. There was a lady and a gentleman inside. I introduced myself, then said:

"Ich habe einen brief von Heidi." *("I have a letter from Heidi.")*

The young man said: "Ist meine schwester in ordnung?" *("Is my sister okay?")* I don't think that Heidi knew she had a brother.

I handed over the letter, which Herr Möller opened. Inside was a photo of Heidi and Jason. I spoke in German, saying that they were planning marriage and they wanted both sets of parents to be at the wedding blessing, by the border. I explained that, if they wished, someone could escort them to the IGB, to a church which overlooked the Iron Curtain. I said that

Heidi, Jason and the Padre would be on the other side of the border, and that they would be able to see them; from that church they would be able to hear each other and, at the very least, wave at each other.

Herr Möller offered me a beer, which I gladly accepted, then another beer. I did joke in German that Jason had sent me to ask permission for their daughter's hand in marriage, which did get a laugh. To say that there were tears of happiness would be an understatement. In a way, it was a time for Heidi's mum, dad and brother to celebrate, and I felt that I had contributed to the happiness of a family on both sides of the Iron Curtain. The wedding was hopefully going to be at Easter, which meant that I might not be escorting Herr and Frau Möller, but someone could be sent if they wished. They declined the escort, saying they would be able to make their own way; they didn't want Stasi knowing their intentions. Before I left, both Herr and Frau Möller hugged me and gave me a photo, saying to give both to their daughter and future son-in-law.

On my return to Münster, I met up with Jason and Heidi in the Pinkus Müller, a brewery pub in Münster. My friend Charlie, myself and the Padre were all there, along with the two of them; we all had something to eat and some real German beer. I handed over the photo, then told Heidi and Jason they had to stand up; I went to each of them and gave them the hug from Heidi's parents.

I was due some leave, and I wouldn't see any of them again.

After that leave, while I was returning to Münster, there was news of a ferry disaster, in which an RAF Corporal and 192 other people lost their lives. Eventually, by summer of that year (1987), I would be posted to Tidworth, then sent on detachment to Belfast shortly afterwards. I didn't tell people about any of the roles I had done; I was in a new environment, with the enemy of terrorism. I know that Heidi and Jason got married that Easter.

Later that year, on 17th August 1987, Rudolf Hess died. This meant that the Soviets now only had the Russian War Memorial as a West Berlin foothold, and I wondered if this would contribute to the dismantling of the Iron Curtain. I hoped that Heidi would be reunited with her parents and brother.

Then, in 1989, Heidi was able to hug her mum and dad. I watched the news with a tear in my eye, because I knew that Heidi and her parents were reunited, and she would meet her brother for the very first time. I remembered what the Padre had once said and I reflected: I felt privileged and fortunate to have been involved.

Chapter 9

Disaster at Zeebrugge

The Townsend Thoresen ferries used by service personnel:

- *M/S Pride of Free Enterprise* (launched in 1979).
- *M/S Spirit of Free Enterprise* (launched in 1979).
- *M/S Herald of Free Enterprise* (launched in 1980; sunk in 1987).

A lot happened in 1987, when I had been privileged to be attached to BRIXMIS. "Never Gonna Give You Up" was the smash hit of the year, as Rick Astley stormed to number 1 in the UK charts, and eventually went on to top the charts in 25 other countries. Conservative Prime Minister Margaret Thatcher won her third general election, after beating Labour by 376 to 229 seats.

Thirty-one people were injured after a car bomb exploded at a JHQ Rheindahlen, which is about 50 miles (80km) from then West German capital Bonn. The IED detonated close to the officers' mess, and twenty-seven West Germans and four Britons were hurt in the bombing. The force of the blast ripped up the road, causing extensive damage to parked cars and surrounding buildings. A statement from the I.R.A. said: *"Our unit's brief was to inflict a devastating blow, but it was ordered to be careful to avoid civilian casualties."*

In the same year, the Intermediate Range Nuclear Forces (or "INF") Treaty was signed by then Soviet leader Mikhail Gorbachev and US President Ronald Reagan. The INF agreement was followed by the first Strategic Arms Reduction Treaty ("START 1") in 1991, which cut the number of long-range nuclear weapons by roughly half.

Toward the end of February, after BRIXMIS, I went on leave, because I needed to use up my entitlement; I remember the Sergeant Major of 27 Squadron saying, "Use it or lose it," so I went on ten days leave.

One of the RCT Section Commanders was Buddy. He was also an instructor, and was very diligent. Buddy took his duties seriously, and displayed great care and conscientiousness in his role. Buddy's favourite military subject by far was drill; there was nothing he liked better than pacing and stamping around on a parade square. He was a very smart soldier, and often an instructor on courses run in 8 Regiment, such as the JMQC (Junior Military Qualifications Course) and SMQC (Senior Military Qualifications Course), both promotion courses being available for RCT and RPC soldiers. Buddy would always be in charge of the drill lessons and, if the wind was blowing in the right direction, we would often hear him bellowing out words of command, even from Coerde (part of Münster). I did consider Buddy to be a bit of a "barrack boy" kind of an instructor; he didn't like getting too mucky out on the training areas, and he always applied camouflage face cream much less liberally than anyone else.

Buddy was due leave at the same time that I was, and he offered to give me a lift, which I gladly accepted. On the Friday we departed on leave, I collected a ferry voucher, which could be exchanged for a ferry boarding pass; it saved the faffing about of exchanging currency from German DM to Dutch guilders or Belgische francs. There were foreign exchanges on the ferries, but they charged quite a lot of money. Only pounds sterling could be spent on board, and because passengers were a captive audience, halfway across the English Channel the exchange rate was against anyone wishing to exchange money, to purchase items on the ferries.

The two main ferry ports that troops used were Oostende and Zeebrugge, in Belgium. The main shipping line or ferry company was Townsend Thoresen, founded in 1968 then defunct in 1987; its successors were P&O.

Buddy, myself and an RCT driver (Smithy) left Portsmouth Barracks just after our evening meal on Friday 27th Feb. We were going to go the following weekend, however our leave was brought forward, due to an exercise. The plan was to get to London, where Smithy and I could catch our respective trains. We made one fuel stop, at a BP filling station in Wankum – this was the last fuel stop on the route to the ferry ports of Zeebrugge and Oostend, where BAOR servicemen and women and their families could use BP fuel coupons, which were very cheap. The coupons could be purchased from unit pay offices, by soldiers who had cars of their own. There was an entitlement that car owners had, and your monthly entitlement depended on the size of your car's engine; if you had a car with a 2.0 litre (2000 cc.) engine you might be entitled to 180 litres per month. Buddy easily filled his Opel Manta for 20 DM of fuel coupons, which would have been the equivalent of about five pounds.

Having arrived at Zeebrugge, Smithy and I had to walk across to the terminal, to buy tickets and board as foot passengers. Not many service personnel had passports, so if there was a border crossing or ferry terminal, we would present a NATO travel order, along with an individual's identity card. The NATO travel order was an A4 sheet of paper, with the usual number, rank, name and unit we were part of. Then there was a section about the Benelux countries, like Germany, The Netherlands and Belgium, which we were likely to travel through to reach the UK. The travel order was usually valid for one year, and the information was written in all European languages. We presented our ID cards and NATO travel orders, and exchanged our vouchers for a return journey. Our ferry was the Townsend Thoresen "Spirit of Free Enterprise". It had an orange and red hull, with white upper decks. The crossing to Dover was about four and a half hours.

There were two bars onboard and somewhere to eat, so having met up with Buddy we ordered a drink. Buddy was a traditional type of soldier, who liked to drink port before a pint; Smithy and I joined him, and we said a toast to absent friends. I learnt a lot from Buddy; he had moral values.

Smithy was going to the Isle of White, and wasn't too fussed about the return journey to Germany; he was on leave for two weeks. Buddy was going on leave to Wales, but it was good of him to go out of his way to drop me off in central London, so I could catch a train to York. No one had mobile phones in the 1980s, so we always made a point of exchanging home telephone numbers, in case there were any changes to timings or travel plans. Buddy and I planned to meet up on the afternoon of 6th March, at Dover docks; I would board as a foot passenger and meet Buddy on the ferry, for our return crossing. I would still have the weekend free before Muster Parade on Monday 9th.

My leave wasn't too eventful. There were the odd jobs which needed doing on the farm, including digging ewes and lambs out of snowdrifts, after very heavy snow. They would shelter from wind next to the dry stone walls, and very often they would perish. Farmers would wrap lambs up in little high-visibility jackets, after treating them for hypothermia. There were also friends and family to visit, and I needed to go and see my sister at work. She had recently completed a fitness course, and was helping to run a leisure centre facility at the Viking Hotel in York, meaning I had free access to use their gym and sauna. I could pack a small day-pack with some clean jeans, shirt and towel, then run into York on the odd evening, before visiting The Roman Bath and The Old Grey Mare for a pint on the way home with my sister.

On Thursday 5th March, the day before I was due to start my journey back to Germany, Buddy rang. My mum answered the phone and passed on a message: Buddy had to remain in the U.K. due to compassionate reasons. This could be a problem. I could use my return train ticket to London, but then I would need to get to Dover. But it was the journey from Zeebrugge to Münster which was going to be a real problem, a distance of 230 miles. There must have been some divine power watching over me, because later that afternoon Buddy phoned again with a solution: he had been in touch with some RCT soldiers from 10 Regiment in Bielefeld; all I needed to do was get my arse to Dover and board the ferry, then find the two lads who had offered to help. I was given the phone number of a soldier called Stuart, and I rang and spoke to him.

"No problems, Mark," Stuart said, "we'll see you on the afternoon, at the ferry information desk." My problem was solved.

There is a saying amongst service personnel: "We don't have problems; we have solutions."

Having changed trains at London, I eventually arrived in Dover. I walked from the train station to the eastern docks, checked in then got on a bus, which dropped foot passengers off next to the ferry. Then we walked up a gangway and boarded the Townsend Thoresen "Herald of Free Enterprise". The weather conditions were quite cold; the air mass was coming from the east, bringing with it cold weather; anyone falling into the sea would fall into a serious state of hypothermia, with their core body temperature falling dangerously low.

Once onboard, I found my way to the information desk, which is where Stuart had asked me to meet him. Soldiers weren't hard to identify. Stuart was a tall, very slim fellow with fair hair and glasses; I seemed to recognize him from one of the RCT squadrons in Taunton. I identified Stuart, gestured then shook his hand.

He said, in a strong southern accent: "Aah, you're the Chunky. Mark, how are you doing, mate?"

There was another soldier with Stuart called Johnna. He was much smaller and a bit rounder, but he was a total gentleman and looked very strong. Both Stuart and Johnna had London accents, and were both experts at the art of creating conversation; I laughed all the way to Zeebrugge. Both had been on leave, but needed to return to Bielefeld for squadron duties.

Having reached Zeebrugge, the drivers of cars and other vehicles were invited to the car decks, to re-join their vehicles. I still needed to leave the ferry as a foot passenger, then meet up with Stuart and Johnna by the terminal buildings. On my way, I could see all the vehicles about to board the ferry I had just left; no one knew about the disaster which would unfold within the next hour or so.

I found Stuart and we departed Zeebrugge, on the N31 toward Gent. Our journey took about four hours. I remember catching the number 8 bus from Principalmarkt, close to St. Lambert's Kirche, to Coerde. It was close to 23:45 when I found my way to the local pub, The Coerde Krug.

Charlie was slouched over the bar, so while he was asleep I quickly drank two of the beers he had stacked up, then carried him back to camp, which was about half a mile away. Charlie gave me a hand trying to get him up the stairs, to the top floor, where I eventually got him to his room, threw his quilt over him, then returned to my room.

About five or ten minutes later, the telephone orderly came into my room. I thought Active Edge had been called, but the telephone orderly said: "No, Mark, it's the CSM, the OC and the Adjutant; they need to know if you're okay."

"I'm fine," I replied.

I got my tracksuit on and went downstairs, to find the CSM and the OC there; the Adjutant was on the phone, in the Company HQ. They were all looking very anxious. The CSM said: "Aah, thank God you're okay."

The OC went on to tell me what had happened, because I was totally oblivious to the events which had unfolded in Zeebrugge. The Adjutant needed to know if there were any other people I knew of who were on the ferry. I told him about Johnna and Stuart from 10 Regiment. He got straight onto the phone to their regiment, to confirm that they had arrived back safely. They thought I had been on the ferry; they were all clearly worried and had gone out of their way to make sure I was okay, and equally that other people were safe. A disaster had happened in Zeebrugge.

The ferry we had been on was the Herald of Free Enterprise, before she left berth twelve, Zeebrugge, on her return journey back to Dover. The ferry departed the inner harbour wall at 19:05 local time, with a crew of 80, carrying 459 passengers, 81 cars, three buses and 47 trucks. She passed the outer mole at 19:24 and capsized about four minutes later. When the ferry reached a speed of 18.9 knots (about 22 mph.), ninety seconds after leaving the harbour, water began to enter the car deck in large quantities – the resulting free surface effect destroyed her stability; in a matter of seconds, the ship began to list 30 degrees to port (left). The ship briefly righted herself, before listing to port once more, this time capsizing. The water quickly reached the ship's electrical systems, destroying both main and emergency power, and leaving the ship in darkness. The ship ended on her side, half-submerged in shallow water, one kilometre from the shore. The entire event took ninety seconds.

The crew aboard a nearby dredger noticed Herald of Free Enterprise's lights disappear and notified the port authorities. They also reported that the bow doors appeared to be wide open. The alarm was raised at 19:37 local time. Rescue helicopters were quickly dispatched, shortly followed by assistance from the Belgian Navy, who were undertaking an exercise in the area. Wolfgang Schröder, the German captain of a nearby ferry,https://en.wikipedia.org/wiki/MS_Herald_of_Free_Enterprise - cite_note-maitland-24 was commended by Prime Minister Margaret Thatcher, and received a medal from King Baudouin of Belgium, for his heroic efforts in rescuing passengers.

The disaster resulted in the deaths of 193 people, many of whom had taken advantage of a promotion in *The Sun* newspaper, offering cheap trips to the continent. Most of the victims were trapped inside the ship and succumbed to hypothermia, because of the frigid water; the rescue efforts of the Belgian Navy limited the death toll. During the rescue, the tide started to rise, and the rescue team was forced to stop all efforts until morning; the last of the people left on board died of hypothermia. Recoverable bodies were removed in the days following the accident. There is a memorial board at St. Mary the Virgin Church, Dover, which contains the names of the 193 passengers and crew who perished.

A salvage operation, conducted by Dutch company Smit-Tak Towage and Salvage (part of Smit International), was embarked upon almost immediately, to refloat the ship. The operation was successfully concluded in late April 1987, allowing the remaining bodies trapped underwater to be removed. The ship was towed to Zeebrugge, then across to the Dutch port of Vlissingen (also known as Flushing), to the yard of De Schelde, where her fate was decided. It had originally been assumed that she could be repaired and continue sailing, however no buyer was found; she was eventually sold to Compania Naviera, Saint Vincent, for scrapping. She was renamed "Flushing Range" and the Townsend Thoresen branding painted over, before her final sailing to Kaohsiung, Taiwan, for scrapping.

She began her final voyage on 5th October 1987, towed by the Dutch tug Markusturm. The voyage was interrupted for four days, when the ships encountered the Great Storm of 1987, off the west coast of Spain, close to Cape Finisterre, when Herald of Free Enterprise was cast adrift after its tow rope parted, before resuming on 19th October 1987. The hull began to disintegrate off the coast of South Africa, on 27th December 1987, and had to be towed into Port Elizabeth on 2nd January 1988, to undergo temporary repairs to allow her to continue her voyage. She finally arrived in Taiwan on 22nd March 1988.

The Townsend Thoresen brand name had inevitably been seen on television and in newspapers around the world. P&O quickly decided to rebrand the company as P&O European Ferries, repaint the fleet's red hulls in navy blue and remove the TT logo from the funnels.

I didn't think that I knew anyone who had perished on board the ferry, but when the names of service personnel began to filter through to units, one of the people I did know was Alan Stedman. Alan was in the RAF, and was a BRIXMIS driver I had worked alongside, only a couple of months previous to the disaster. He had been telling me he was due to be posted, but would be going on leave at some stage before Easter of that year. He was 31 years old.

Chapter 10

Belize

As Pioneers, we did get to travel to a lot of countries throughout the world. Have you ever heard of Belize? There was always a detachment of Pioneer soldiers in Belize.

Belize is a beautiful part of the world, in Central America, and is part of the Yucatan Peninsula. To the north is Mexico, to the west and south is Guatemala and to the east is the Caribbean Sea. The coast of Belize had mangroves and no beaches, but there were islands off the coast, called "cayes", ranging in size from a football field (like English Quay) to a long strip of land (like Ambergris Caye). All the cayes formed a sort of archipelago, a chain of small islands of coral and limestone, and form the second largest barrier reef in the world (the largest being the Great Barrier Reef, off the coast of Eastern Australia). The beaches on the cayes are almost like a rough, gravelly sand. There is a type of seaweed which gets washed up onto the sand and sandflies by the million, which can be a hazard, because some sandflies can leave people with a medical condition called leishmaniasis, where a sandfly bite becomes ulcerated; the condition needs to be treated by a series of intravenous injections over a period of time.

The weather conditions were normally very hot and humid; it gets very sticky. There are three seasons in Belize: the dry season, when it is baking hot every day; the wet season, when it rains heavy downpours most days; and the hurricane season. During the wet season, each downpour lasts a few minutes, sometimes half an hour, then it very quickly dries up again; all of this rain and evaporation causes thunderstorms. After a period of time, the whole process repeats: rain, thunder, then dry, and on and on. The rain is very often accompanied by thunder. Some of the thunderstorms were amazing, and at night-time each lightning bolt lit up the whole sky; you could see for miles. During the hurricane season everyone had to gather up loose items, and lash buildings and vehicles down. Coconuts had to be disposed of, because if they were picked up by hurricane-force winds they could quite easily cause structural damage to a solid wall.

Inland there are highways. Unlike our dual carriageways, these were more like hardstanding tracks, with the odd bit of concrete road here and there. Many people in the UK moan about the potholes on British roads – well, the potholes in Belize were like caves! At certain times of the year, land crabs would start to migrate across the roads, toward the sea, to spawn – some of these crabs were the size of dinner plates.

The landscape is rainforest, for as far as you can see, and there is a range of mountains called the Maya Mountains, which stretch into Guatemala. Most of the geology consists mainly of limestone, meaning there are hundreds – possibly thousands – of caves, called cenotes, many of which are filled with water. Many cenotes were linked, forming huge networks of flooded caverns and caves. Jacques Cousteau was a French naval officer, explorer, conservationist and filmmaker; back in the 1970s, he discovered that many of the cave networks inland were linked by caverns and underwater caves, which extended out to the Caribbean Sea.

There are literally whole hidden ancient cities and other treasures, beneath the canopy of the rainforest: settlements and pyramids built by Mesoamerican cultures, such as the Maya. Mesoamerican cultures were the people who, from the mid-Mexican region all the way down through Central America, were indigenous and native to that area of land. The

Maya were one such Mesoamerican civilization, which existed from about 1500 years BC and had almost collapsed by 1519 AD; the Spanish conquest of the Maya, led by Pedro de Avarado, paved the way for the Spanish, but witnessed the fall of the Maya.

The Spanish had a protracted conflict during the Spanish colonization of the Americas, in which the Spanish conquistadores and their allies gradually incorporated the territory of the late post-classical Maya states into the colonial viceroyalty of New Spain. Until then, the Maya occupied a territory which is now incorporated into the modern countries of Mexico, Guatemala, Belize, Honduras and El Salvador. The conquest began in the early 16th century, and is generally considered to have ended in 1697. Spanish weapons included broadswords, rapiers, lances, pikes, halberds and crossbows; they also had old-world technology, such as a functional wheel, horses, iron, steel and gunpowder. They were also extremely susceptible to old-world diseases, against which the Maya had no resistance; I suppose this could have been a form of biological warfare.

Maya pyramids were built to resemble mountains to worship the gods; the more important the god, the higher the pyramid was built. In Maya culture, human sacrifice was the ritual offering to the gods; blood was viewed as a potent source of nourishment for the Maya gods, and the sacrifice of a living creature was a powerful offering. This included the most precious offerings; even a child was not exempt from sacrifice.

The Maya had an interesting way of settling disputes between one village and another; rather than going to war over a dispute, the Maya played a ball game called Pok-ta-Pok. This game would eventually evolve into modern-day sports like volleyball and basketball. Pok-ta-Pok was also played by the Aztecs. The rules of the game would differ from one region to another, but it was generally played on a court with a halfway line, which players were not allowed to cross. At each end were steep stone walls with a thick, horizontal stone hoop; the aim was to score by getting the ball through the stone hoop. If the ball crossed over the line, into the other team's half of the court, then they had the advantage; if your team dropped the ball then it was the other team's advantage; it was a no-contact ballgame. The ball was made from solid rubber, and was about the same size as a modern handball, but about the same weight as a bowling ball. This game was not only a way of settling disputes between people within a village, it was also a way of identifying and selecting warriors. The winning team could also decide who would be sacrificed to the gods.

In addition to the Mayan and Creole people, there were a group of people called the Mennonites. The Mennonites trace their origins particularly to the so-called Swiss Brethren, an Anabaptist group which formed near Zürich, on 21st January 1525, in the face of imminent persecution for their rejection of the demands of the Zürich Reformer Huldrych Zwingli. They are a religious community; part of the Protestant Church which rose out of the Anabaptists, a radical reform movement of the 16th century Reformation.

Mennonites are still found in many countries of the world, but are concentrated most heavily in Central America, the United States and Canada. Mennonite villages are spotless; they build each other's houses by hand, out of timber, and I remember a Royal Engineer Lieutenant being amazed, and somewhat shocked, commenting on the very high standard of craftsmanship.

Not far from San Ignacio there was a Mennonite village. Each house had its own beautifully laid out garden, with very bright, brilliant white fencing and a gate to each garden; the garden paths were paved, rather than concrete. There were no cars; each family had horse-drawn carts and wagons, which were highly polished. The Mennonites were expert farmers, who could turn the desert into a rich and fertile land.

The rainforest is nearly always referred to as "jungle", and there are two types, "primary" jungle and "secondary" jungle. The primary jungle has fully-grown trees and a very high canopy; the ground is fairly clear because the sunlight can't penetrate to generate new growth. Secondary jungle is new jungle which has just started to grow, often after logging; the sunlight reaches the ground and the vegetation races to grow, so at ground level the forest is very thick.

There are all sorts of species of tree, but the Black Palm is one tree that all soldiers there know about. It is an innocuous-looking plant, which conceals horrid spikes that shred your skin; the military call them "bastard trees". These aren't big trees – the trunk may only be a few inches in diameter, about the same thickness as the average flagpole – but these trees have very sharp, prickly spikes all over the trunk. Very often, as it was getting dark, you might lose your balance and grab onto anything to stop yourself from falling; if you grabbed a Black Palm, the first thing you shouted would probably be "BASTARD!" hence the name. This Black Palm could be quite a hazard, because it was like having lots of deep papercuts all over your hand, and due to the heat and humidity in the jungle, any cut would likely become infected almost straight away; troops were advised not to shave, because even a shaving cut could cause an infection. Fortunately, there was an antibiotic powder we were issued with, which could be used with a dressing to reduce the risk of infection.

The rainforest is rich in life. It provides ecosystems and habitat for all sorts of animals, many of which are on the edge of becoming extinct. Some creatures could be potentially harmful, but others I considered to be just daft – such as the coati. This adorable animal, which inhabits parts of South America, Central America and North America, is about the same size as a large house cat, and they are harmless; closely related to the raccoon, the coati have a ringed tail, though unlike the nocturnal raccoon, which is active at night, the coati mostly gets its sleep when it is dark.

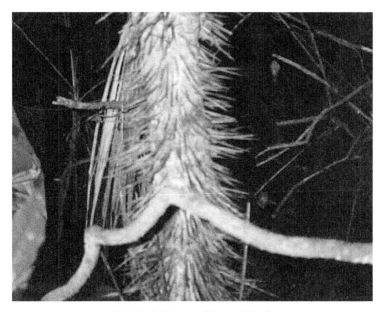

The Black Palm, or "Bastard Tree".

Coatis live up in the canopy of the forest, which the trees form; they would often live in trees close to areas frequently occupied by troops. These animals turn treetops into their bedrooms, even building comfy twig-and-leaf nests in branches for their babies. Soldiers have been known to return from patrols to find a coati occupying their sleeping area, possibly because they feel safe from predators. As a coati sleeps, it tucks its long nose into its belly. Soldiers would often report a coati sat next to them on a log, and there were even reports of these animals sitting on the shoulders of soldiers.

During the day, the coati is all about snacking. Coatis usually eat insects, fruit, rodents, lizards and small snakes, but from time to time they would scrounge any food they could, and often beg for items in a ration pack. On several occasions soldiers would be eating the fruit biscuits in their ration packs, only to find a coati desperate to get a biscuit; they also loved processed cheese. In the wild, coatis would use their long, flexible noses to probe gaps between rocks and search under piles of leaves for food.

Female and baby coatis eat, sleep and travel in packs of about thirty; at age two, the males leave to live on their own. In groups these animals are chatty; they click, grunt, whistle and bark as they forage for food. While it may not be as well-known as its raccoon relative, the coati definitely lets you know it's there; they would be a good indicator that something dodgy might be about to happen – natural alarm systems.

The role of British forces in Belize was to deter a Guatemalan invasion. Prior to 21st September 1981, Belize was called British Honduras and was British sovereign territory. Guatemala did not recognize the new nation of Belize, because of a dispute over the former British colony, claiming that Belize belonged to Guatemala. If the Guatemalan troops got too close to the border, there was always a Harrier Jump Jet on call to provide FGA (fighter ground attack). It could take off from part of the international airport – called Charlie Delta – and be anywhere along the border within minutes. It would hover between the observation posts and the Guatemalan forces, and bow by dipping its nose; the Guatemalans would very quickly withdraw.

There was also a secondary role, which was to assist the BDF (Belize Defence Force) in locating cartel drug plantations. The cartels or drug gangs would plant cannabis and grow other drug-producing vegetation, which grows very quickly in a warm, humid environment. Once a plantation was identified, a crop sprayer was sent out. This was a very basic, single propeller aircraft, which had armoured plates around where the pilot sat. Very often, the crop sprayers would return riddled with bullet holes.

The maps of Belize were workable; in fact, some were very good, and had the gridlines, numbers and all the other useful information printed on them. A lot of the maps were very basic, though, and very often had no gridlines, although there were the easting numbers along the top and bottom of the map, and northings on each side. When issued a basic map I would draw in the gridlines, making it easier to identify 4 and 6 figure grid references, and easier to plot grid bearings; we would use anything with a straight edge, then line that edge up with the relevant grid numbers and draw in the gridlines. The maps would include a key to identify symbols, and some maps had magnetic information, which was quite useful. There would normally be a green sheet indicating rainforest, while roads, villages, creeks and rivers were also on the maps, though I found the contours, and other information about what we thought were hills, quite useful. Sometimes, we would arrive at what we believed to be a knoll or a round hill, only to discover it was a Mayan pyramid. Some tracks were marked on the maps, but only the very well-used ones; tracks were often reclaimed by new growth of vegetation. If you were patient enough, you could be lucky enough to witness seeds sprouting, and leaves and shoots growing.

You could never die of thirst in the rainforest; there were thousands, probably millions of vines, which looked like thick ropes, hanging down from the canopy; it just needed a chop from a machete and cool, crystal-clear water would flow, to very quickly fill a water bottle – if a milky fluid flowed out, we would avoid and move on to another vine.

The rainforest is not a peaceful place. In the daytime, there would be a troop of howler monkeys, howling at other troops of monkeys, miles away. When it started to get dark, at about 17:00 each day, the howler monkeys would start to quieten down. Then, just as you thought it would be getting quiet, thousands of tree frogs would begin a chorus, chirping all night until first light. It was constantly noisy and there was never any peace.

Much of the time in the jungle was hard work. Normal routine was demanding, but at least we could build a fairly comfy "A frame" – a one-man shelter of a platform or folded-over poncho sheet between two frames, each forming the shape of an A, one at each end of the poncho; we then had to find two long poles, which were placed along each inside edge of the poncho, to form what looked like a stretcher. The ends of each pole would be placed over each of the A frames, and the shape of each A would force the longer poles apart, tightening the bed of the poncho. It would only work if we could find wood which wasn't rotted, and was strong enough to support our weight. An alternative was to string a hammock between two trees – but selecting two trees wasn't as easy as you might think; what might look like a solid tree might be dead with a rotten trunk, just held up by vines and branches of other trees.

Having found two sturdy trees, soldiers would clear the whole area of leaf litter and twigs – this was done to clear away any nasty things which might bite. There was a type of powder we were all issued with, which would keep insects and other fauna away from us, and this powder stunk. The powder had to be dusted all over the space we had cleared, while insect repellent and powder would be squirted and dusted onto the straps and lines suspending our hammocks. When lying in a hammock, we needed to be about two feet off the ground, to keep away from things which might crawl, sting, slither or bite. It wasn't just the Guatemalans and drug cartels who were hostile; the whole environment could kill us.

All soldiers were entitled to two weeks of R-and-R. We had the option of returning to the UK, which most of the pads did, or for the single soldiers there was Cancun, which was a few hours' bus ride north, in Mexico. Many soldiers also went to the United States, usually Florida. On my first tour, three of us had the same R-and-R, and we decided to opt for Orlando. On my second tour, three of us decided to go somewhere out of the way, up in the Rocky Mountains; I prefer cool environments, and Belize is very hot and humid, so a cool place was perfect.

All three of us boarded a TACA (Trans American Continental Airways, though the RAF nicknamed them "Take a Chance Airways") Boeing 737 jet, and flew to Denver in the state of Colorado, then got on a coach to Glenwood Springs. None of us had booked a hotel; on arrival at Glenwood Springs, the bus dropped us off close to a youth hostel. The people who owned the hostel had lots of rooms – some were for families, others were dormitories, and there were several single and double rooms.

The gentleman on reception said that they only had a few guests taking advantage of the cycling available, but during the winter they would get packed with guests for the ski season; Aspen (the main skiing attraction in Colorado) was only a short drive away. He told us his kids had grown up and one of them, called Sandy, had joined the US Airforce; the other, Emma, helped to run the hostel, and took people on tours during the ski season. There were plenty of activities to do, and we were charged just 30 bucks (dollars) each, for 12 days! A bargain.

The owner of the youth hostel and his wife (Benjamin and Susan) were about the same age as my parents, or possibly just a bit older. Ben had served in the Vietnam War (November 1955 – April 1975), and he was incredibly happy to have three British soldiers staying with him. Vietnam has rainforest, and many skills used by the British in Belize may have been passed on by the Americans – for example, they had also built A-frames to sleep on. The British and American choice of personal weapons was also the same: the U.S. troops used the AR-15 (M-16) in Vietnam, as did many British units in Belize. I don't think the British used the M-60 machine gun, but we had the GPMG.

There were bars, restaurants and all sorts of shops in Glenwood Springs, but Ben decided that we should all go to a restaurant bar called Doc Holiday's, just over the road. It was the sort of bar that tourists might use, and the menu had all the normal stuff you might expect to see on any pub menu.

Benjamin, Susan and Emma treated us all like we were part of their family, and they each had awesome qualities. On the last day of our R-and-R, Ben insisted on taking us all back to the airport in Denver. He even gave us the youth hostel number, and said we needed to ring him, so he knew that we had arrived back in Belize safe. It was clear that Ben had held the rank of WO, because he cared to the point of worry.

Our own WO, CSM Taff Thomas, was going to fly from the UK to visit us all, and would be with us for one week, during which there was a long weekend. He was another soldier who cared. Our Platoon Commander summoned all the Section Commanders for a briefing in his office; we needed to decide where to take the CSM for a couple of days, over the long weekend: we had a choice of Cancun, Chetumal (also in Mexico) or San Pedro, which was the easy option; there was plenty of accommodation and we could get a boat taxi.

The boat taxis were very quick; they were speedboats, which could fit six of us in, a couple of slabs of beer and kit. Boat taxis were plentiful on the way out, but getting back could be dodgy, even if you booked one to bring you back to Belize City. Another way of getting to San Pedro was to make friends with the Port Squadron RCT; they had landing craft. I was friends with some of the RCTs I knew from 8 Regiment, and it was more than probable that Taff Thomas would know the same people.

The day of our CSM's arrival was here; the VC-10 was on schedule and would land shortly after lunch. I was instructed to go to the airport and pick up the CSM, then take him to the WOs and Sergeants' Mess. Once he had his room all sorted, I was to show him his temporary office, which we had borrowed from the RAF; it was only a small office, with two chairs, a desk and a ceiling fan in the middle. It had a swing door, which had mozzy netting panels; there was a walkway directly outside the office door. The CSM would be pleased with his office.

A driver and Land Rover picked me up from our accommodation, to go and pick up the CSM. The airport was only a fifteen-minute drive away. Once through the main gate, we passed Charlie Delta, then turned right onto a rickety, old, yellow-looking road. The Yellow Brick Road was more of a muddy track, which created a shortcut to the main airport terminal. It joined two tarmac roads, and when travelling along the track, would pass one end of the runway; we turned onto the road from just opposite the Belikan Brewing Company. The Yellow Brick Road was often patrolled by the RAF Regiment, and many troops from Airport Camp would use the road for PT sessions, as well as its use as a BFT route. Eventually, the Yellow Brick Road would need to be rerouted, so that the runway could be extended to accommodate much larger aircraft.

By the time we had arrived at the main building of the airport, the VC-10 had landed. The main terminal doubled up as the arrivals and departures lounge; any passengers arriving on civil flights followed a one-way system, picked up baggage from a pile, then continued on their respective journeys.

It took about half an hour until the CSM came through into the arrival hall. He was wearing a pair of chinos and a polo shirt, and he was carrying a suit carrier and a holdall. He had a strong Welsh accent when he spoke. "Hello, Mark, it's good to see you."

I braced up and said: "Good to see you too, sir. The transport is this way."

"Relax, Mark."

I had known the CSM for a long time; he had been my Section

Commander in 8 Regiment, after Cpl. Pugh was posted. As a Staff Sergeant, he was an instructor at the Royal Military Academy, Sandhurst. Instructors at Sandhurst were the cream of instructors, Army-wide; they only took the very best of the best – and our CSM was one of them.

The following morning, all of our platoon were formed up outside, awaiting the arrival of our CSM. He already knew where his office was going to be.

When our Platoon Commander arrived ten minutes before the CSM, I had a brainwave. I discussed my plan with our Platoon Commander and he agreed. The CSM would need an orderly, or a runner – a "go-fer" – and his runner for the day was Jacko. He was a Private (very soon to be a L/Cpl.) but he was already a PTI. Having Jacko was a bit like having a disciple. He would eventually become an excellent JNCO and SNCO. I got Jacko to go and get some foot powder, then I said:

"Right, Jacko, come with me."

Jacko followed me to the CSM's new office. I asked Jacko to switch off the ceiling fan, got the spare chair and placed it under the fan. Once I was stood on the chair, I asked Jacko to pass me the foot powder, and I gently emptied the whole container over each of the four fan blades.

I heard someone say: "Quick, Mark, the boss is here."

I quickly jumped down, put the chair back and got Jacko to follow me. Jacko took his place in the platoon and stood easy.

As the boss brought the C.S.M. around the corner, I shouted: "PLATOON... PLATOOOON... SHUN!"

Immediately, the lads sprung to the position of attention.

Then I shouted: "IN OPEN ORDER... RIIIIGHT DRESS... EYES FRONT... CENTRE AND REAR RANK STAND AT EASE."

The boss went into his office, which was only next door to the CSM's office, and the CSM marched toward me. I did a left turn to face him and we inspected the lads; they were all smart in their tropical combats. The CSM stopped and had a chat with each and every one of the lads; he knew them all by their first names. He was suitably impressed and addressed all the platoon. When some RAF lads passed by, I looked toward them and thought:

Yes, lads, this is what a real Sergeant Major looks like.

The CSM then made his way into his office and Jacko followed him. I told the RAF lads to stop, and come back and watch what was about to happen; in a way, I felt a little mean. As the CSM entered his office, I heard him say: "Get that fan on, Jacko; it's like a sauna in here."

There was a look of horror on everyone's face, when a moment later what appeared to be two snowmen came out of the office, spluttering and covered in powder. Jacko was muttering:

"It wasn't me, sir! It was that twat over there."

I was lucky; the CSM had a very good sense of humour. He laughed and said: "I will get my revenge, Corporal Nichol." I was a little bit worried. Later that day, in the RAF bar, I did say that I owed him for all the pranks he had played on me over the years. The CSM could have gone to the WO's and Sergeants' Mess, and spend each night in there, but he tipped his hat to the SWO (Station Warrant Officer) and mentioned that he would like to use the RAF Bar and Mess on his final night.

It was Thursday afternoon, and the CSM wanted to know where the lads would go in their spare time. There was a bus stop just outside the main gate, where the Freddy Krueger bus would pick up troops and take them to Belize City. On the way there, it would stop at Raul's Rose Garden, which was a knocking shop. Lads would get off the bus, to a cheer from other lads on the bus, with a blush and a smile.

The CSM, being curious, asked where they were going.

"For a shag, sir," I replied.

He asked: "How much does that cost?"

"Twenty-five bucks," I said.

The CSM asked: "Have you ever been in? What's it like?"

I told him that Jacko, Dave and I have been in once or twice. There is a bar and a green door at the far end, which is where you go for twenty-five bucks' worth.

"Is it legal, Mark?"

"Oh, yes," I said. "There was a fella from 24 Squadron who went in there for his two weeks R-and-R, sir."

"Two chuffing weeks?! Did he catch anything?"

"No," I explained, "the ladies in there are checked by the MO (Medical Officer) for infections once a week, and they get the thumbs up. Antibiotics and other pills are free; it's almost like a healthcare plan they have. Some ladies are from other Central American countries, others are from the States; they are all looked after and paid very well. I think some of them may be from cartels, but the RMP and Snowdrops (Royal Military Police and RAF Police) are aware of and monitor them."

When the CSM smiled, I said: "Would you like a look inside, Taff?"

"Ooh, no, I don't want to be lowering my standards, Marky."

Having dropped off the troops who wanted twenty-five bucks' worth, we continued on the bus into town. There would only be two or three other stops, to drop off staff who worked on Airport Camp. The Swing Bridge was our stop, where we all got off and went to our first port of call, The Upstairs Caffe – or, as it was commonly known, The Upstairs NAAFI. Having had a rum and coke or a Belican Beer, we would then walk around to the Belleview Hotel. Curfew was at half-past midnight, so we usually got the last bus back at midnight.

On that Friday morning, the CSM went with the boss to visit lads at Holdfast, then bring them back to Airport Camp for the long weekend.

Some lads went to Cancun and others to Chetumal. The CSM was happy with going to San Pedro.

The boat-taxi ride took about half an hour to 45 minutes, depending on whether you got the fast or slow speedboats; if you went by landing craft, it would take about an hour and thirty minutes. We already had three boat taxis booked, and hotel rooms in San Pedro. If ever the lads did anything daft or funny, we would fine each other a "slab", which was a crate of beers which resembled a slab. They were very cheap, at eight bucks a slab. We must have had at least twelve slabs of beer to wade through once we got to San Pedro, and even full ice boxes; we only needed cash for the boat taxi and meals, which would normally be burger and chips.

By Friday afternoon, we were all loaded up on a truck to take us to the boat taxi, then head out to San Pedro. The weather was going to be hot for the next few days and our Platoon Commander Lt. Sollit was already there; he had been flown out by the RAF the night before, and sorted all the rooms out.

There were lads there, happily drinking rum and coke, which didn't really float my boat; I was happy with Belikin Beer, which to be honest wasn't a bad pint. It was a local beer, brewed by Belize Brewing Company; their brewery was just on the doorstep of APC (Airport Camp). The brewery was founded by Eric and Barry Bowen in May of 1969, as Cervecaería Hondureña, then in 1981 the brewery became independent and the name changed. Many lads called it "Bellyache Beer". The only other beer available was Schlitz, which was an American beer brewed by the Joseph Schlitz Brewing Company, Milwaukee. There was also Miller's (also American), in bottles with screw-caps. I always took a slack handful of alcohol cleansing wipes from the medics, because I preferred to drink beer from the bottle, but the crates were not stored in clean conditions, as neither were the cans; a quick wipe would get rid of any bacteria. It was the same with stims bottles (Coke, Fanta and Sprite): if you didn't wipe around the top of the bottle, you could get ill with something quite nasty; or at the very least you wouldn't dare pass wind, in fear of a full unload or follow through.

San Pedro had its fair share of bars and hotels, one of which had live sharks swimming about; the bar itself was on a wooden pier, about fifty metres long. Halfway along the pier was the bar, which had a seating area inside an "attap". An attap is traditional housing found in Brunei, Indonesia, Malaysia and Singapore; it could be a dwelling or a bar. Named after the attap palm – parts of which provide the wattle for the walls and the leaves with which their rooves are thatched – these dwellings can range from huts to substantial houses, and they are proper, sound structures. Brunei is where British forces attended the Jungle Warfare Instructors Course, and they would eventually apply the knowledge of attap construction to Belize, to construct buildings in the jungle – and, of course, bars.

On the other side of the bar was an enclosure which housed the sharks, with seats around it. There were several species, including blue sharks and white tip sharks. The bar had the sharks in a sort of captivity, to study them, and scientists would take blood samples from the sharks, to research and develop human medicines and cures for life-threatening medical conditions. There were even horseshoe crabs, with blue blood. Dr. Brady Barr, a famous reptilian and crustacean biologist, discovered components within the blood of these crabs which is now used in medicine to treat Parkinson's disease, begging the question of whether it could be used in the fight against nerve agent poisoning, alongside atropine.

We arrived safe and sound in San Pedro, where Lt. Sollit was waiting. He even had a beer in his hand, but sadly only a cheap pair of shades – not like the rest of us, with our Oakleys.

The CSM was a bit disappointed that he wouldn't organize an event, but we had done it for him. He went snorkelling and did some SCUBA (self-contained underwater breathing apparatus) diving, down to ten metres. Very often, adventure training brings out hidden talents, courage and skills in people; you often discover qualities about yourself and others. You also see a different, more pleasant side to people.

Despite the heat, there was always Baldy Beacon, where I would sometimes run the ranges for various shoots and for training purposes, such as PT. It was a place where I felt more at home, because of the cooler conditions. Jungle training was below the canopy, near Blue Creek, where jungle survival courses and other jungle-related courses were available – maybe not necessarily the sort of course people would volunteer for, but they were good courses nonetheless. I found having other instructors around incredibly helpful, because we could learn from each other.

Even as an experienced map-reading instructor, there were other courses available that I wanted to do, and one such was a jungle navigation course; it taught me a lot.

Shaun Parker, a Royal Engineers S/Sgt. (Staff Sergeant), and Royal Highland Fusilier Corporal Soup Campbell taught me a lot about navigating in the jungle, using the features rather than tracks, which were unreliable. It was a non-tactical course, so minimal weapons were needed; the only firearms we took were with a BDF Corporal. He was a jungle guide, but had never been in this area before. I spent a week with them, learning new navigation skills.

There was a suitable location in the Toledo District, in the southern part of Belize, where creeks that would flow into the Rio Grande. Not far from San Miguel was an ideal location, with attap buildings, for us to establish a base. Also nearby were some ancient ruins and a site of antiquity called Lubaantun, where the daughter of British adventurer and writer Fredrick

Albert Mitchell-Hedges had discovered a crystal skull, in 1924.

Primary jungle is firmly well-established rainforest, where the ground isn't too hard to walk, due to the lack of sunlight not triggering new growth, but secondary jungle was a bit like walking through a forest in the U.K., with bramble and blackberry bushes shredding your ankles; it can be time-consuming hacking your way through this type of forest. On one occasion in the training, we had travelled on foot through thick secondary jungle on a compass bearing; there was a hill I needed to get to – or at least a ring contour, giving the appearance of a small hill or a knoll – but on the way there was an obstacle. We only needed to travel for five hundred more metres (half a grid square) and we would have nailed it; there was, however, a ravine, which was marked on the map as a re-entry between two spurs. To get to the other side we needed to go uphill, across the ravine, then come back down the other side. We had no rope, and attempting to jump across would have ended in casualties from falling. So, we hacked down a bastard tree and placed it between a pile of stones, so that it would be visible from the other side; we also marked our maps. I estimated that it might take up to three and a half hours to reach our required position on the other side of the ravine. Naismith's Rule is a rule of thumb which helps hikers when planning an expedition, by calculating how long it will take to walk an intended route, taking into consideration any uphill sections of a walk. It was devised by the Scottish mountaineer, William Naismith, in 1892. But his rule doesn't really work very well in thick secondary jungle.

We had probably gone no further than fifty metres uphill, when Soup said, in his strong Scottish accent:

"Slo doon, Mark. Slo doon, pal."

I slowed down. As he approached me he said: "What's that?"

He was pointing at a stone sculpture. I marked its position as accurately as I could, then took a closer look. It appeared to be a man with a jaguar headdress, sticking out of the ground. This was strange, because there were no buildings either on the map or on the ground. Still, we continued uphill, keeping the ravine to our right.

We eventually came across what looked like a stone ramp, at the head of the ravine. We all stopped, and I was surprised by how quiet it was; all we could hear was the wind in the trees. I marked our position on the map.

"Let's continue up, Mark," Soup said.

We all recorded the bearing and the back bearing, and continued.

Secondary jungle was turning into primary forest, and walking became a bit easier. Then, after about twenty metres of walking, we all just suddenly stopped. There was another statue.

Shaun came to the front and said: "We may have to bin the leg of our route taking us to that knoll, Mark; we may have found something."

As well as being an instructor, Shaun had also done training as a topographer, and had a vast knowledge of map-making skills; he was an expert in the subject. He brought from his Bergan two fifty-metre tape measures. I asked him what he was carrying them for. He said: "I'm a surveyor, Mark; it's what we do."

We were at the base of a pyramid, and this god must have been very important, because it was huge; the BDF soldier was quite shocked.

We had a radio with us, and transmitted a message with our position. We gave them what Shaun thought might be the rough size of the base: it must have been just over thirty metres along one edge. We were given instructions not to go into any buildings.

We set up a base and camp, with hammocks and bashas, then did some exploring. The whole thing did look like a knoll, with trees growing everywhere, but it was a pyramid which had been reclaimed by the rainforest, and left undiscovered for hundreds of years. There were other buildings with flat rooves, and we couldn't help but look inside some of them; in one we found a skull and several bones: possibly the remains of a family. We tried to speculate on possible theories of why they perished.

Within two hours, a team from Belmopan had been flown in, but they had to trek through thick secondary forest, via the same route to that we had taken. It was interesting to see that the forest was already reclaiming the track we had made earlier that day.

News travels fast, and on returning to Airport Camp the Station Commander already knew all about our expedition. The sad thing was that none of us got mentioned for having found what turned out to be a Mayan town, not even the BDF soldier (who was from Belize). The whole site became a Mecca for explorers, archaeologists and others wanting to plunder artefacts; there were even ancient history representatives, conducting a study into the theory that ancient aliens once visited the Earth. I was thankful to Shaun, Soup and the remainder, for the privilege of joining them.

Chapter 11

Big John Smith

"Do not underestimate the determination of a quiet man."

Iain Duncan Smith.

The BFT (basic fitness test) is a three-mile run, broken down into two parts. The first part is a one-and-a-half-mile run, as a squad of soldiers, and must be completed in fifteen minutes. The second part of the test is to run back one-and-a-half miles, but this time it is an individual effort. A soldier's age will determine how much time is permitted to pass the second part of the BFT. The timings to pass are as follows:

MALE		FEMALE	
AGE	TIME	AGE	TIME
29 and under	11 mins 30 sec	29 and under	12 mins 45 sec
30 – 34	12 mins	30 – 34	13 mins
35 – 39	13 mins	35 – 39	14 mins
40 – 45	14 mins	40 – 45	15 mins

The dress for the BFT was a PT vest, lightweight trousers, putties and DMS boots; no kit and no weapons. Eventually, though, the dress code changed from boots to trainers.

Having passed the test twice a year, the results were recorded. If a soldier failed, he or she would have a second attempt one week later, under the same conditions. If a soldier failed a second time, the soldier would be referred to the doctor or MO (Medical Officer). If the MO found no medical condition the soldier would have to get up at daft o'clock each morning to take part in remedial PT. A week later, they would attempt the test again and hopefully pass.

Big John Smith (yes, you read correctly, John Smith; everyone called him "Smudge", so John Smith became known as a Smudge Smith) was a big, gentle, giant lad who loved his beer; he preferred bitter, rather than the girly stuff that other people drank. His favourite bitter was Boddington's Best, and he could drink quite a lot of the stuff. When Smudge spoke he had a lisp or a short tongue, but with a very broad Bolton accent he actually sounded like the famous steeplejack Fred Dibnah. He must have weighed in at about seventeen, possibly eighteen stone; he was an endomorph, but he was incredibly strong.

Our unit was 187 Company RPC, and our CSM was a WO1 (when a squadron or a company are away from the main hub of a unit, the Sergeant Major is usually a Warrant Officer Class 1, rather than the traditional Warrant Officer Class 2). There are squadrons and companies throughout the Army which are independent of a regiment; an example of this might be 33 Independent Field Squadron RE, in Antrim, Northern Ireland: it was away from a major unit, like a regiment. 187 was a bit like that, because it was away from 23 Group. The CSM was my old mucker Tom Appleyard, who had been the CSM of 144 Company.

Uncle Tom liked to let the troops go about lunchtime every Friday. The normal routine was to get up, have breakfast then block jobs, ready for the CSM to inspect. While he was inspecting, the soldiers would be doing PT, normally in the form of a BFT. Any failures – and there would always be a few – would be on guard duty that weekend, either that evening, the next day or Sunday. So, there was an incentive to pass the BFT: you got away early, and if you had been in turn for duty the CSM would delete you from the guard and insert the BFT failures.

Poor old big Smudge was nearly always on duty at the weekends. The only way Smudge got out of doing any duties was when he was on detachment. Uncle Tom would love it whenever Smudge returned to Tidworth; he knew he would have someone for his duties. The thing about big Smudge was he was never late for any duties or any parade, and when everyone else had knocked off for the day, on normal weekdays, Smudge would volunteer to stay behind and finish off any unfinished work.

Smudge couldn't pass a BFT. He had passed one back in his basic training, and one or two since, but no more than that. I wanted to change this, so I formulated a plan. I spoke to Bach, who was now a Staff Sergeant and the Chief Clerk. Bach hmmed and aahed, then gave me his seal of approval.

The following Friday I took the BFT. There was only a handful of lads in station; the rest were away on detachments. As predicted, Smudge failed the BFT by about a minute. He was put on duty that Sunday, so he had Friday night and Saturday night free to go for a pint or two. There was a pub called The Ram in Tidworth, and Smudge and I had our tea, then at 18:30, along with two other lads and Bach, we took a stroll to the Ram. Smudge got the first beers in.

The landlord said: "Usual, Smudge?"

Smudge replied: "Oh, aye, 'n two more, 'n sum o' that lager stuff, please."

Smudge sank his pint before I'd even got mine to my lips. Then he said: "Another un, please."

He took a sip, then placed his pint on the bar. He took his time with this pint, but he had still supped it before I was halfway down my glass.

Then it was my turn to order the beers. "Same again, please," I said, adding: "what part of 'take your time, Smudge' don't you understand?"

Smudge said: "Ooh, erm, sorry, I will slow down. I'm just a bit thirsty, that's all." Then: "Same again please, Phil."

It was the same every time we all went out. It must have been entertaining for Smudge, watching us walking to the Chinese then back to camp; he would be fine, while the rest of us were staggering all over the place.

Throughout the week we would follow a training program, then on the following Friday we did the BFT, and Smudge would fail again and be on duty again.

One Tuesday evening, Smudge and I went to The Ram. It took me ages to drink my beers, while John ordered more; I had two beers stacked up. Smudge said: "Come on, Mark, lad, sup up. We're off to t' Chinese, an' it shuts in ten minutes."

I managed to drink my beers, dribbling most of it down my top, then we got outside and Smudge led the way. He knew a shortcut – if there was food involved, he would know every shortcut. Smudge was running, moving at a fair old pace, and I was struggling to keep up with him. There was a huge, green, metal fence surrounding a football field, and we needed to get to the other side, then we would be at the Chinese in no time; the other option was to walk to the end of the field then through a housing estate.

Smudge said: "I'm off ower, Mark."

It was like he had vaulted over it, yet I was huffing and puffing; Smudge hardly broke a sweat. We got to the Chinese just in time and ordered our takeout. Smudge broke into a jog, which developed into a run, on the way back to Kandahar Barracks; I had never seen him move so fast.

After I had stuffed my face with spring rolls, special curry and fried rice, I said: "Why can't you do that on a BFT Smudge?"

I went to my room and got into my pit. I was now in the final part of formulating my plan.

Wednesday morning, we opened up the Armoury next to the Guardroom and started cleaning weapons. While the lads were stripping, cleaning then assembling weapons, I took a walk to the cookhouse and had a chat with one of the chefs; I made up a story that he would be on a driving job, and wouldn't be back until about 09:30, so could I please order a late breakfast for Smudge. The chef said: "Of course." All I needed now was four cans of beer. I hid the beer in a cool place.

Thursday evening we had a bull night, in preparation for the CSM's inspection the next day. After the bull night, we didn't go The Ram; instead, we went and had a beer in the NAAFI.

"Ready for your BFT in the morning, Smudge?" I said.

"Erm, aye, I am. I'll try 'n' pass it."

"Fingers crossed, Smudge," I said, "fingers crossed."

The following morning I got up, then went into the dorms to get the lads up. Most of them were already up and ready to go for some breakfast. Smudge was sat on his bed, winding his putties around his boots.

I asked him: "How do you feel, Smudge?"

Smudge replied: "Aye, I'm all-reet."

My plan was to not let him go for his breakfast, but to get him to drink the four cans of beer I presented him with. I said: "Drink these tins, Smudge."

As I was talking to Smudge, he appeared not to be taking any notice; he was already busy drinking the four cans of bitter. "At 09:30 the chefs will be expecting you; they will be cooking a big, fat, hairy full English breakfast with your name on it."

Now I had his attention. "Wot? A massive breakfast, all for me… at half nine?"

I said: "Yep, and happy birthday, Smudge: you're thirty years old today."

Smudge had forgotten his birthday.

When the troops all formed up there must have been twenty of them. The CSM also joined us, along with an officer and a Sergeant. I turned the squad to face the direction we were going, then shouted:

"BY THE FRONT... QUICK MARCH."

With all the troops in step, we headed off. After about fifty metres, I shouted: "BREAKING INTO DOUBLE TIME... DOUBLE MARCH." This was only a gentle jog; the person doing the test should be able to hold a conversation with minimal discomfort.

After a while, I would shout: "BREAKING INTO QUICK TIME... QUICK MARCH."

The BFT would follow that pattern until we reached the halfway point, sticking to the fifteen-minute time limit. As we reached the halfway point, I broke the squad into quick time, and crossed the line with twenty-five seconds to spare. The squad broke up and formed up on the line. I handed over the stopwatch to another PTI, who had a bike in the back of the safety vehicle, so that he could cycle back and record the time and age of each individual on the register.

When all the troops were lined up, I shouted: "STAND BY... GO!"

They were off.

I ran back with Smudge and two others. I kept saying: "Don't slow down or walk, Smudge. Keep going!"

I would like to think that I offered some inspiration to the other lads, as I said: "Don't let me down, lads... Keep going... Not far now."

As we reached the finish line, the PTI with the stopwatch shook his head to indicate that Smudge had failed; he had crossed the finish line in

11 minutes and 40 seconds. He was gutted.

Then I said: "How old are you, Smudge?"

He replied: "Thirty today."

I smiled: "Then go and stand with all those who have passed; you still have twenty seconds left in your age group! Then go get your breakfast; I will meet you in the cookhouse. Well done."

That was his first pass in a long time.

On arrival in the cookhouse, the OC, CSM and several other SNCOs were there to greet him. To say that Smudge was happy was an understatement. Bach was in the cookhouse expecting us. He said:

"Once you've all had your breakfast, go and get changed into civvies; we'll take John into Salisbury and get him shitfaced. The bus leaves in an hour."

It did make me think that all John needed was encouragement and a better incentive. After that weekend, Smudge decided that he would go for the odd run around the BFT route twice a week. He would never fail the BFT again.

Chapter 12

Prince of Wales Company (Jam Boys), Welsh Guards.

Ascension Island is a volcanic island; its lower slopes and western side are made up of volcanic ash, with little vegetation. Green Mountain rises to a height of 859m at the centre of the island, and is itself rich in vegetation, like a tropical rainforest. The island is almost in the middle of the Mid-Atlantic Ridge. To the west is Brazil, about 2,250 kilometres away, and to the east is Angola, which is about 1,600 kilometres away.

The sand isn't the white sand usually associated with tropical beaches; it is very dark – almost black sand and ash. The island was discovered by the Portuguese navigator Joo Nova, on Ascension Day 1501, and was occasionally visited thereafter by ships. In 1701, William Dampier was wrecked on its coast, and during his time there he discovered the only spring of fresh water the island contains. The island was first occupied in 1815 by the Royal Navy, when they incarcerated Napoleon in his exile on nearby St. Helena; they did not want any rescue mission to use Ascension Island as a base to work from. A small town, named George Town, was built on the northwest coast; it was the best bay for the ships, but was some six miles from the only source of fresh water, in Dampier's Springs. The island was placed under the direct rule of the Admiralty, and was run as if it were a ship; it was governed by a naval captain, under the command of the Admiral Superintendent at Gibraltar.

After the death of Napoleon, it was realized that it would make an ideal depot of stores for the Navy, and it was visited once a month by mail steamers from the Cape. The island became an important cable station, and Cable and Wireless maintained a permanent office there. After the First World War, the island finally passed from military to civil control. The Colonial Office made the island a dependency, to be administered from the much more populous St. Helena, in 1922.

An airbase was built on the island, which became an important refuelling station for the USAF and the RAF. Its strategic significance and importance became apparent during the Falklands War campaign, as it became an important staging post for ships and aircraft. Ascension Island also became a good staging post for UN troops to go into Angola.

In 1995 we were deployed on Operation Chantress. I can remember being on Ascension Island; we were waiting to fly by C130 Hercules aircraft into Benguela, Angola. While we were on Ascension, we met up with a Pioneer (Jasper) who was stationed on the islands. Jasper worked in the stores unit and was attached to the RAF; if there was ever anything that you wanted, Jasper was the one to go to. Jasper met us on our arrival and took our platoon to our accommodation; we would be there for three nights, in a dormitory which looked more like a hut in Belize, but it did the job. All the other units which were part of 9 Supply Regiment were accommodated in a hangar; the Welsh Guards had accommodation at the other side of the airfield.

The CO insisted on a two-can rule, meaning that service personnel could consume alcohol, but only two cans. On our first evening on Ascension, Jasper offered to go and get some slabs of beer. Each slab contained twenty-four beers and cost £6; each Pioneer soldier donated a fiver and we ended up with £135. Jasper wandered off with the cash, then returned an hour later with a four-ton truck – in the back were thirty crates of beer, all freezing cold. I asked Jasper if there were any cool boxes with ice. Jasper said: "Gi' me twenty minutes."

He was on a mission, and twenty minutes later we all had loads of ice. It was a nice way to acclimatize to the hot weather. We had recently completed a tour in Belize, so a bit of sunblock and a dress code of a pair of shorts rolled up into the appearance of a nappy order was sanctioned by our Platoon Commander, and seconded by our Platoon Sergeant.

That evening, we saw six Welsh Guards walking toward us. One of them, Glenn, came across and very politely asked if he could buy a couple of beers. Glenn was the Section Commander, holding the rank of Lance Sergeant.

Reuben, one of our Section Commanders, said: "Nah, bring your lads over and come have a beer." We all stayed up until breakfast the following morning, just nattering away, having a good laugh and drinking beer. Jasper had never had so many visitors and he loved it.

We all had to keep away from one part of the coast, where there were endangered animal species living, and Green Sea Turtles due to hatch. One of Jasper's tasks was to build a section of fence around where the turtles had laid their eggs, and I don't think he could have done it on his own, so a slack handful of Pioneers and some Welsh Guards gave Jasper a hand; the following day, they had constructed two hundred and fifty meters of fence from six-foot piquets and barbed wire. A guardsman then asked Jasper if he could get some signs and some olive paint. By teatime of that day, the guardsman and a Pioneer had made triangular signs and painted them red, with the words *"DANGER, MINEFIELD. KEEP OUT!"* painted in yellow. The signs did look very convincing, and they were fastened to the fence at regular intervals. The two lads had even painted lots of the empty beer tins olive green with yellow lettering, giving them the appearance of mines, and planted them. I don't think the public go to Ascension Island on holiday, but if they were to, the fence they might have come across would have deterred them from going onto the beach.

On our last day on Ascension we discovered that our platoon would be providing a section to the Royal Engineers, and the two sections would be attached to the Welsh Guards, to provide defence for the UN locations in Lobito. By this stage we had attended briefings with the Welsh Guards and got to know quite a few of them. They were the Prince of Wales Company First Battalion, often called "Jam Boys". Glenn had told me that Prince of Wales Company was made up of the tallest soldiers in the battalion, and historically they were issued an extra ration of jam because of their size. These lads were indeed very tall, and our Platoon Sergeant became the smallest in the company. CSM George Evely would tease him at mealtimes: "Don't forget, eat all your tea; you'll never grow up if you don't."

The flight to Angola was by a "Herky Bird" (Hercules C130). They were the ideal aircraft, because they can operate from unprepared landing strips. All of our vehicles were on the RFA (Royal Fleet Auxiliary) Sir Galahad, just off the coast of Angola. The ship was an LSL (landing ship logistic), and it was waiting to dock, but couldn't until we had secured the docks area. There was no hostility when we landed in Angola, and we even had coaches provided by the UN to take us to Lobito docks. In addition to the docks, there were several locations needing to be cleared and secured, which we would operate from.

An old, abandoned warehouse was taken over by the Royal Engineers, called Cassa Invicta. This warehouse was more rubble than building; girders were hanging down, there was masonry everywhere and most of the roof had collapsed, but the RE turned it into a functional home. There was also a huge warehouse that the Welsh Guards took over. It had a railhead, where trains would be loaded with grain. The grain was mostly dried maize, and there were millions of sacks of it in this warehouse, as the location was a UN and World Food Programme food storage facility.

About halfway through the tour, a train loaded with grain left the warehouse. We opened the gates, where hundreds of the local population had gathered in hope of food or water donations, but we were forbidden to give out any food. One of the locals ran toward the back of the line of flatbed wagons, where some maize was leaking out of a sack; the man had a container which looked like a cup, and he ran alongside the train catching the maize. One of the security guards on the train saw this and shot him. The saddest thing was that someone ran to the now lifeless person and stole his flip-flops; it appeared that a person's life in that region was totally worthless.

I had on lots of occasions given water bottles away – we all did – and sometimes I would be criticized for it. There would be thousands of crates of water that we could help ourselves to, but the UN would tell us not to give any food or water away. If I gave a bottle of water to a stranger or a child, then at least that person would feel better. I know we couldn't help all the people, but we could certainly make a difference to a few, even if only for one hour.

One of the most amazing things we witnessed in Angola was when the RE had a load of containers, which could be put on the back of trucks. Each container had plant machinery which would turn gopping water into cool drinking water, working on a process called reverse osmosis. Mucky water was sucked out of a stream, a river or even the sea and treated, then pure drinking water would spurt out of the other end, through a fire hose at high pressure. The nicest thing I saw was a Sapper with a hose under his arm, pointing it at a load of kids and us. "Water on," he said, then a torrent of life-giving water was squirting over us and the kids. The spray formed a rainbow, which one of the kids pointed at in amazement. I later discovered that the Sapper was Sully, the first Royal Engineer I met with Charlie and Bach, at Long Marsden. I think he should have received a commendation, because he put smiles on a lot of people's faces; those people lived for every day, because tomorrow they might not be there.

Just over halfway through the tour, several of us were stood around a "Puffing Billy": a galvanized steel dustbin full of water, engineered to heat it. The water heater was a tubular device attached to a chimney, with a petrol fuel tank; the petrol would drip down lit, then ignite the petrol in the bottom of the tube. Lighting the Puffing Billy was very entertaining, and this task was usually given to the chefs; they would get up each morning to light the Puffing Billy. Very often it would backfire, and we would see lads shuffling toward us with soot all over them. In the past, many soldiers lighting these boilers would come away with burns which needed treating, but the chefs had by now all mastered the art of lighting the Puffing Billy.

It was morning and I had just had a nice cold shower. We were going to set up security of a hotel and hospital in Lobito. All the lads had their weapons and we were just waiting for a bit of breakfast, which was boil-in-the-bag, heated by the Puffing Billy, and a brew. BFBS was on the radio, and the song "Wake Up Boo" by The Boo Radleys was coming over the airwaves. The Boo Radleys were a British indie band, and the track became their biggest hit, both in the UK and internationally. *"Wake up, it's a beautiful morning,"* rang out the chorus – but somehow I didn't think that I was going to have a good morning.

Glen approached me and said: "What the chuff have you done to upset George?" He meant the CSM. George Evily was a big fella, who had been an instructor at the School of Infantry, in the Brecon Beacons. There was rumour that he had been a mercenary in some of the neighbouring countries to Angola; politically, it was a very unstable part of the world.

One of the officers, Lt. Morgan from the Welsh Guards, asked me the same question: "The Sergeant Major is like a bear with a sore head this morning! What have you done to upset him?"

"I can't think of anything, sir," I said.

Lt. Morgan said: "Well, you need to think quick, Corporal Nichol; the CSM is after blood."

A few moments later the CSM passed, looked toward me and said: "The shit is this deep and you're in it."

Just then, Sergeant Dawson appeared and said: "I have to warn you for orders, Mark: 14:00 this afternoon you need to be back here, outside the CSM's office."

I was wracking my brain. I wondered what on Earth I had done, but couldn't think of anything. Was it the other night, when I took some of the Guards and Pioneers to one of the safe bars? Surely not.

At the hospital, I said to Glenn: "I'm going to be in here later today, aren't I, Glenn?"

To which he replied: "Yep."

Stuttering, I said: "Glenn, you're not helping! The CSM is a beast… H-h-he has killed people, Glenn!"

"Yeah, I know," said Glenn. "Don't worry, Mark; we've all been on the receiving end of George's wrath."

At 13:30, a UN Military Police Land Rover carrying two monkeys (Royal Military Police, or RMP) came to take me back. This was going too far now.

One of the RMP said: "Are you Sergeant Nichol?"

I said: "No, I'm Corporal Nichol."

The RM.P Corporal said: "Ger in the back."

I got in and they drove me back to where the CSM was going to kill me. Both RMP were shaking their heads, tutting and laughing, but I didn't see what was funny. They stayed with me, while I waited for the CSM to arrive; I was sweating like a daft soldier who was about to attempt a spelling test. The CSM kept the RMP and I waiting.

Then Sergeant Dawson came past and said to the RMP: "Come with me, lads, for a cool drink. Nichol, remain stood there… and to attention, if I were you!"

What seemed like hours passed, then suddenly I could hear George shouting; I must admit, I nearly defecated involuntarily. He came around the corner and stopped in front of me.

Then he said: "Come on, then, tell me what you've done."

I said: "I might have taken some lads to one of the bars at the end of the spit, sir."

"Oh, you did, did you?" he said.

I went quiet, then the CSM and the two RMP marched me into the OC's office. I was marking time along with my two RMP escorts for ages, until eventually the CSM shouted:

"STEADY… HALT!"

The OC looked up, read my number out and said: "Are you Sergeant Nichol?"

I said: "Er… erm, no sir, it's Corporal Nichol."

The OC repeated: "Are you Sergeant Nichol?"

At that point, I could see the shadow of the CSM and my RMP escorts' shoulders bobbing up and down as they laughed.

Then the OC stood up and handed me the rank slide of Sergeant… and shook my hand.

Then CSM shook my hand and said: "Don't worry, Sergeant Nicholson; we all love you really."

I released a breath I had been holding all morning and grinned.

I still had to continue as a Section Commander until I was posted. Lieutenant Solit was avoiding me, but I caught up with him and Glenn.

I said: "You two have no doubt heard of a *school* of fish, a *herd* of cattle and a *flock* of birds?"

Glenn said: "Yeah, Mark. Get to the point."

I said: "Well, you lot are a bunch of twats!"

Equilibrium was restored.

One of the tasks we had was to remove human remains from some of the sewers. Before the UN could enter Angola, the recognized government had to invite them. The UN then demanded that all bodies must be removed from the streets before they deployed.

On one patrol, "The Beast", as he was known, said in a very Welsh accent: "What is that smell?"

My section 2IC looked at me; we knew exactly what that smell was. I called Glenn over and informed him. I said I needed to investigate some of the drains, which we could see down inside.

Glen said: "I'll set up a security cordon."

I got out my torch, and shone it through the metal bars of a grate leading to the sewers. I could identify a hand with fingers missing, a foot and a round object, which may have been a head. Then I went across to another drain, only to discover a ribcage. We cordoned off the road, as Glenn got on the radio.

We couldn't open any drains, because of the threat of booby traps. Specialists were sent to our location; crowds formed as they arrived. In total, they recovered close to twenty-eight sets of human remains. Some limbs or even heads were unaccounted for, and they could only identify sixteen; twelve people had been totally mutilated. It was the same in other streets: remains of people had been stuffed into drains, in an attempt to clear the streets of human remains.

Not long before the end of our tour, our section, along with Lt. Solit, were tasked with escorting a coachload of children for UNICEF. There were three compounds we had to visit – Andulo, Kassenge and Huambo –

to pick up a total of twenty-three children, many of whom were emaciated through lack of nourishment. All the kids were orphans, and were being looked after by organizations such as Save the Children; these organizations relied on donations to provide food and medical care for children. Many children in Angola lived in sewers, to keep away from gangs, which would exploit them to smuggle diamonds, drugs and weapons. Having accounted for all the children, the coach, escorted by two United Nations Snatch Land Rovers, drove toward the capital Luanda.

There were several creeks on the way, with bridges which needed to be cleared of any mines; one bridge had mines scattered all over the bridge decking. These were former Soviet Union mines, and some were bounding mines, meaning that once triggered a small charge of explosives would launch the mine up to waist height before it detonated. Our vehicles came to a halt.

We had all listened to a briefing about what to do if an event like this happened. Glenn's fireteam took up non-aggressive positions around the coach, and all the kids were sent to the back of the coach; my fireteam was ready to clear then secure the bridge, along with some Sappers. Lt. Solit took a Pioneer, a Welsh Guardsman and a Royal Signals interpreter – weapons were slung behind them, so as not to present themselves as barriers – and the three soldiers walked toward the six militia who were holding the bridge. One of the militia approached Lt. Solit. Our orders to open fire stated that if a person's life was under threat, lethal force could be used; two of my soldiers provided top cover from the front Land Rover, each with a light support weapon (LSW). The rest of the militia stood on the bridge, presenting themselves as targets, with their weapons pointing toward us.

Lt. Solit liked to smoke and he had some cigarettes. He removed his cheap sunglasses and took the pack of cigarettes out of his pocket, offering them to the leader of the militia. The leader accepted, taking just one from the packet. Lt. Solit gave the rest of the packet to the leader, then in English asked if the mines could kindly be removed; the interpreter conveyed the conversation in Portuguese. The leader of the militia turned around and shouted to his men to remove the mines, which they did. Lt. Solit displayed very valuable qualities and reduced the risk of conflict; he was polite, kind, efficient and smart.

Angola is a country about the same size as France. It is rich in terms of its natural resources, such as oil and diamonds, but isn't the sort of place people would want to visit on holiday – perhaps it could be one day, when the conflict ceases. There are some hidden treasures, including miles of beaches to the south, going into Namibia. Our tour in Angola would eventually come to an end, but what a tour!

We returned to Ascension Island, where Jasper was waiting, and remained there for three nights; everyone had the same accommodation. I instructed Glenn and the other Section Commander to bring their lads to where we were. Once there, Jasper lined us all up then said:

"I was expecting you all, so I did some concurrent activity: I saved the beer that we didn't get through the last time – and I've pre-ordered fifteen more slabs! There is plenty more if we need it."

Jasper got a donation from everyone; we all gave generously to the fund. We did use the cookhouse facility for breakfast each day, but the rest of our meals were beer, and enough barbecue to last forever. All the Guards joined us – even the CSM and the OC. It was a good way to end a tour, and the saddest day was when we all had to go home. It was a privilege to have served with the Jam Boys.

Chapter 13

Northern Ireland

"Patience and diligence, like faith, remove mountains."

William Penn.

The Royal Pioneer Corps had two globe-trotting companies – 187 Company and 518 Company – and there was a very good network of Pioneers all over the world, including Northern Ireland. They had a range of tasks and roles, which included support for the Royal Engineers, themselves support for the infantry regiments. Pioneer sections and platoons had a valuable range of skills, they were nearly all drivers, and most were assault Pioneers. A lot of the JNCOs were instructors, some lads were chefs and some even had trades. There was a saying that if you were a Pioneer (or Chunky), you were a jack of all trades but a master of none. Yet many soldiers from other regiments would often rely on Pioneers to help them out, and providing we had enough resources we could generally help people and fulfil our tasks. Bob's Bar in Belize, for example, was a favour, and was built by RAF, a couple of RE and Pioneers; even the Station Warrant Officer (SWO) did a bit of digging.

"Operation Banner" was the operational name for the British armed forces operation in Northern Ireland, from 1969 to 2007. Northern Ireland is a fascinating part of the British Isles, and it is blessed with beauty and history. There are six counties:

DOWN – main city Belfast;

ARMAGH – main town Armagh;

FERMANAGH – main town Enniskillen;

DERRY/LONDONDERRY – main city Londonderry;

TYRONE – main town Omagh;

ANTRIM – main town Antrim.

The Troubles in the province date back to August 1969, when the UK government sent troops to impose control. They lasted for about thirty years and would claim more than 3,500 lives. Many people would argue that the trouble in the province started in 1919, then settled in 1920. This period was called the Anglo-Irish War, between the Irish Republican Army and the British forces, with the Royal Irish Constabulary (RIC) – the police force in Ireland, active from 1822 until 1922, when the whole of Ireland was part of the United Kingdom.

Some people even claim that the trouble in Ireland went as far back as the 1500s, when King Henry VIII was on the throne, but this may be open to debate. The Protestants would often target the Catholics, and this led to violence, so British troops were sent to protect the Catholic population. Troops were initially a welcome sight to the Catholics, but the honeymoon period was short, when the IRA claimed it was themselves who should provide protection. The tables were turning, and the Catholic population soon tired of the Army presence, beginning to resent the British troops patrolling the streets of Northern Ireland.

Gunner Robert Curtis of the Royal Artillery was officially the first of 705 British military fatalities in Northern Ireland. Gunner Curtis was deployed to Northern Ireland on 5th January 1971, under the command of 32nd Regiment Royal Artillery. During the first week of February 1971, there was major violence in many Irish republican areas of Belfast, when the British Army launched a series of searches for I.R.A. arms and ammunition. Rioting in the republican area of New Lodge escalated and reinforcements were called for; 156 Battery was ordered into the area. Because mobs of rioters were threatening the bordering unionist Tiger's Bay area, the Battery was deployed along the interface to block them. A large crowd gathered at the junction of New Lodge Road and Lepper Street, and a troop of soldiers from 156 Battery, including Gunner Curtis, were deployed to disperse the crowd. As the troop moved to the junction, they were attacked with a barrage of stones and bottles by the mob and deployed in "riot formation", with shields as protection. Subsequently, a nail bomb was thrown at the soldiers, and in the aftermath of the blast the crowd split, allowing a gunman to fire a long burst of automatic fire from a submachine gun, probably from the base of Templar House. The crowd then reformed, allowing the gunman to escape. Gunner Curtis was hit by a ricochet, which passed through the shoulder opening of his body armour (flak jacket), penetrating his heart; he died almost instantly. Four other soldiers were wounded, one seriously. The modern terrorist was born.

There were five main key events during the Troubles, though there would have been a trigger for each of these events:

- CIVIL RIGHTS CAMPAIGN (1964 to 1972):
  A number of initiatives emerged, which challenged inequality and discrimination in Northern Ireland.
- INTERNMENT (1971 to 1975):
  This is where suspects could be arrested and detained without trial at Long Kesh, more often referred to as "The Maze".
- ULSTER WORKERS COUNCIL STRIKE (1974):
  A general strike which took place in Northern Ireland, between 15th May and 28th May 1974, during the Troubles. The strike was called by unionists who were against the Sunningdale Agreement, which

had been signed in December 1973.

- HUNGER STRIKE (1981):

  The Irish hunger strike was the culmination of a five-year protest by Irish republican prisoners in Northern Ireland (HMP The Maze). The protest began as the blanket protest in 1976, when the British government withdrew Special Category Status for convicted paramilitary prisoners.

- PEACE PROCESS (1993 to the present):

  Talks between the leaders of the two main Irish nationalist parties in Northern Ireland – John Hume of the Social Democratic and Labour Party (SDLP) and Gerry Adams of Sinn Féin (SF) – continued. These talks led to a series of joint statements on how the violence might be brought to an end. The talks had been going on since the late 1980s, and had secured the backing of the Irish Government.

There were other important events, such as the "dirty protest" (March 1978 to 2nd March 1981), which was part of a five-year protest by Provisional Irish Republican Army and Irish National Liberation Army prisoners held in The Maze, and a protest at HMP Armagh Women's Prison. Pioneer soldiers were sent in to clear up the excrement which had been smeared on the walls of each cell.

On one tour I did of Northern Ireland, a Royal Marines Commando needed a very big favour. I was on detachment in Kinnegar, just north of Belfast, where there was a huge ordinance depot; Pioneers provided security for the Guard Force, with regular patrols along the shore road and into Hollywood. Quite often, other troops could come into the Guardroom and brew up, while they were waiting to collect items to take back to their units. I remember a Royal Marines Commando Section Commander entering the Guardroom; he appeared to be under stress. He booked his two Snatch Land Rovers in, then said:

"Are you Mark?"

"Yes," I said.

"A Pioneer from Lisburn said you would be able to help."

One of his lads had lost four rounds of 5.56 ammunition. SA-80 magazines held thirty rounds, but troops in Northern Ireland were often only issued twenty rounds. They had been patrolling part of south Belfast, and were travelling back to Lisburn along the M1 motorway, when the young Marine's magazine fell out of his SA-80, off the back of the Snatch vehicle and onto the motorway. A truck behind them ran over the magazine, and the rounds spilled out all over the road. The patrol stopped on the hard shoulder, went back to where it had happened and salvaged the mangled magazine and spring, but could only find sixteen rounds. When soldiers lost operational ammunition there was usually an inquiry and a soldier would face disciplinary action, receiving a minimum £50 fine for each round of ammunition they had lost; this Marine was looking at a £200 fine. His Section Commander and I were not going to let that happen.

All I needed was the batch number. The Marines in the patrol were unloading their weapons in the unloading bay, and their Section Commander had sent them to the NAAFI for a break. I asked how long they had, before they needed to be back in Lisburn.

He said: "Not until later this afternoon; we're picking up some paperwork. I can't believe I took him on patrol with a magazine which wasn't fitted correctly." When going on patrols, soldiers had to be supervised clearing then loading their weapon; commanders were even given a script to read from, to ensure weapons were loaded, unloaded and cleared correctly. There was a notice to that effect behind each loading/unloading bay.

I asked if their boss back in Lisburn knew about the incident, to which the answer was no. I said: "Let's go for a brew – or is it a 'wet' you Marines call it? We'll see what we can sort out."

The Marine who had lost his ammunition was quite anxious, but we did put his mind at rest. I said: "Give me an hour and you'll have a fresh mag and the four rounds you're missing." I had access to surplus operational ammunition, and I was able to help.

Helping someone in need has its rewards. The following Friday, a car drove into Kinnegar; the occupants were the two Royal Marines. They booked in the car then opened the boot, to reveal two crates of beer. They came into the guardroom and thanked us for the help we had given them. They didn't need to repay us, but it was a way of showing appreciation.

There was also a Pioneer detachment at HQ3 Infantry Brigade, in Armagh. Drumadd Barracks were on the outskirts of the town, on a hill. Steve Wake was one of the Royal Signal Corporals in the stores; he also had to open up the Armoury daily, so that troops could withdraw or hand in weapons. Steve was a very hardworking fella, who would have done anything for anyone. The RSM of the unit was WO1 RSM Stan Wise, a Geordie fella and a gentleman. The RSM would do an inspection of the accommodation, then go on his rounds every Friday morning. Steve and I shared a room, and we made sure the room was spotless.

One morning, the RSM walked in and said: "Good morning, chaps. What's happening today, then?"

Steve said: "It's the Friday ammunition drop, sir."

"Ooh, all those heavy boxes, Steve. Well, have a good day, chaps," said the RSM.

I went to do some chores for my boss, then met up with Steve in the NAAFI. He asked me: "What are you doing for the rest of the morning, Mark?"

I replied: "Not much now. I have an escort job on tomorrow."

"Would you be able to give us a hand offloading the ammo?"

"Of course I will, Steve." It was going to be heavy lifting for an hour or so, but it would be a good bit of "fizz" (physical exercise).

"See ya down there in fifteen minutes, Mark," Steve said.

Ammunition boxes are quite heavy, and they were on trucks; there is no way that Steve could have done this on his own.

After about twenty minutes, the RSM appeared on his rounds and said: "Hey, Steve, d'ya remember when I was the SQMS and we used to get all those ammo boxes to stack in that cellar? I used to hate doing the ammo run, Steve: all that lifting; it just seemed to go on forever. D'ya remember that, Steve?"

Steve was huffing and puffing. Between stacking a box, he stopped and said to the RSM: "Allow me to take you on a trip down memory lane, sir. Tec yer hat off, put yer stick down and come and give us a hand."

And so the RSM did just that: got stuck in and gave us a hand.

Dave Tablock was a Pioneer at the same unit I was attached to; he was also one of the storemen. Every once in a while, we would get clearance to go to Portrush, where there was a campsite on Dunluce Road. We would normally arrive there in the summer months, in late afternoon, put up tents and roll out sleeping bags. Dave and I were then all set to walk into town, get something to eat then have a pint or two, before hitting the sack back at the campsite. On one occasion we took one of the officers; Lieutenant Davies was a very intelligent gentleman in the Royal Signals, part of the Brigade HQ.

After a few pints on the Friday evening, we returned to our tents. The following day, the idea was to do a coastal walk, part of the Ulster Way. It was safe, we had completed a route card and we would visit the Giant's Causeway, walk up to Aird Snout, round to the Giant's Boot, then visit the exhibition centre. While we were wandering around the hexagonal-shaped stones, Lt. Davies commented how spectacular they looked, and that he wondered how the stones were formed.

Dave Tablock answered: "Well, sir, fifty-million years ago the whole world was run by giant bumblebees; these stones are fossilized honeycomb the bees made."

Lt. Davies looked on in wonder.

On the way to the exhibition centre, he asked me: "Were the stones really formed by bees, Mark?"

During tours of Northern Ireland, there was a lot of hostility aimed at the RUC and the armed forces, but even in the midst of that hostility there was always something that would make you smile. Lt. Davies made us all laugh.

One tour that I did in the province was in Belfast. I had recently returned to the U.K. from Berlin and was sent to Belfast on detachment. I was required to escort several trucks to Bessbrook, from Antrim.

Bessbrook was an old mill, built around the Industrial Revolution, which ran from 1760 to sometime between 1820 and 1840. It was used to produce linen and textiles. The mill was constructed from granite, in stages, between 1845 and 1880; it is now a B1-listed building. The architect was W J. Gililand. Bessbrook witnessed a lot of I.R.A. activity during the Troubles, but the IRA only launched only one successful attack on Bessbrook Mill itself: in April 1987, a mortar strike injured three soldiers in the base's vehicle park; there were no fatalities. The IRA killed its last soldier in Bessbrook, in February 1997, when a sniper shot a soldier through the neck while he was talking to a villager at a road VCP (vehicle checkpoint).

At 11:00 hours on Sunday 8th November 1987 (Remembrance Sunday of that year), a bomb exploded in Enniskillen, County Fermanagh. The

Provisional Irish Republican Army, or PIRA, had planted the bomb; it had been set to detonate by a timer at exactly 11:00. The explosion took place near the town's war memorial during a Remembrance Sunday ceremony, which was being held to commemorate British military war dead. Twelve people were killed and sixty-three were injured.

Our day started early; trucks were lined up with escort vehicles at the front and rear of the convoy. The journey was good, as we followed the main route on the M1 toward Belfast, continuing along the West-link, down toward Lisburn then Portadown, then onto the smaller A and B roads to Bessbrook. No vehicles had followed us and there was nothing peculiar to report. It was Sunday.

We arrived at Bessbrook in time for breakfast, after which we had to wait in the old mill, along a corridor next to the Ops Room, in case we were needed. Bessbrook was the busiest airhead for helicopters in Europe, and aircraft were in and out in quick succession every day.

I was asked to help the Padre set up his chapel, in the attic of the mill. We set up all the chairs, got rid of items which weren't needed, then went back to the Ops Room. At about 10:00, the Ops Officer asked me to take some troops up to the chapel for the remembrance parade. I took more troops as they arrived, and by half-past ten the chapel was full. I was then required back in the Ops Room.

The bomb in Enniskillen detonated as the silence was being observed. The blast reduced all the buildings in the surrounding area to rubble.

Just after 11:00 there was a lot of activity over the radios; aircraft were starting up and troops were forming up, ready to board helicopters.

The Ops Officer said to me: "Go up and give this note to the Ops Warrant Officer in the chapel."

Once in the chapel I handed over the note. The Ops WO read it then took troops away… then more left, then more. What had just been a packed chapel was now almost deserted; there was now only the Padre, myself and one other Sergeant. Still, the Padre continued with his service; he didn't stop or pause once, he was so diligent.

I had to wait until that night before we escorted the same trucks back to Antrim, then returned to Belfast.

It wasn't all work; there was time to enjoy and visit parts of the province. Like the Mourne Mountains, a granite mountain range in County Down. The highest is Slieve Donard, standing at 850 metres above sea level. A circular wall was constructed to enclose a water catchment area, which supplied water to the reservoirs, and to keep in livestock. Construction of the Moure Wall began in 1904 and took about eighteen years; it is twenty-two miles long. Many people do the walk without a map – you can't really get lost; it is a circuit. And a fantastic walk.

Chapter 14

CTT

It was my turn to be posted. My posting order arrived and I was going to a CTT (cadet training team) in Nottingham.

Before I was posted, I needed to conduct one last respirator check in the Respirator Testing Facility (political correctness for the "gas chamber"). As it was my last week, I decided that the CO, RSM, OC, CSM and squadron officers all needed to have their respirators checked, too; I needed to talk to the Training Wing Sergeant Major and ask him for permission, and to keep things quiet. I even managed to get the Padre involved.

This was going to be fun, as it was going to double up as my going away do. I quite liked using the chamber itself. It was a small, cube-shaped brick building, and I knew I would struggle to get everyone inside, so I had the option of using a 12 x 12 olive-green tent. I got some lads from the squadron I was in to help me put up the tent, to use as an alternative chamber. We had enough tables and chairs, all transported in by Rat Fan (he reminded me of Roland Rat; he was my driver. He had a Westcountry accent and was a typical Trogg; he could drive anything on the road. If ever you needed transport, then Rat Fan was the man.

The lads and I laid the tent out, just as I wanted; I even had tablecloths and place names, with respective cap badges printed on them. I had ordered and collected the CS tablets and lighting fuses (a bit like waterproof matches), then sealed the tent, ready for that afternoon. No one was allowed to drive (except Rat Fan, with his truck), so I had to arrange transport for everyone to be taken home.

The senior members of the regiment all arrived on time, and I asked them all to get into "dress category three" (Noddy Suits on, but with hoods down). Then I shouted:

"GAS! GAS! GAS!"

Now they were all in Three Romeo, with respirators on and hoods up. I checked all participants, even the Padre, who wouldn't normally do anything like this, but he got stuck in; the Padre and two assistant NBC instructors were my disciples for the afternoon.

I went into the main testing facility, lit the tablets to get an acceptable concentration of CS gas, and invited each of the participants into the chamber, which was now very foggy. They all had to shake their heads and jump up and down for about thirty seconds, then they would do decontamination drills. I must admit, I was a bit disappointed that no one had any leaks. Then I led everyone outside, with their respirators still on, and asked them to face into the wind, to blow away remaining CS powder.

I took them into the makeshift chamber, one at a time, and stood them all behind their respective chairs and tablemats. It was a cheese and wine party; I could see their shoulders going up and down as they all chuckled. I asked the Padre for grace, then invited them all to raise a pre-poured glass of port to absent friends. This was the funny bit: I told them that there was still a high concentration of CS gas, and any attempt to unmask would result in them displaying the effects of it. As they all kept their respirators on, I got them to practice drinking drills. Then I got them to practice eating drills. The Padre looked as if he was crying through his lenses, and at first I thought he had a leak – but it turned out he was laughing. Once I was happy, I told them to enjoy the cheese and biscuits, and wade through eight bottles of red and six bottles of white; any leftovers would find their way to the Padre's chapel.

The day I was posted came around very quickly. It was just before Easter of 1999. I was required to hand G1098 items of kit back to the SQMS – items such as webbing, sleeping bag and other bits and bobs. On arrival at my next unit I would be required to visit the new stores, to sign for items of G1098 equipment; I would keep hold of that kit until my next posting, possibly in 2021.

I had been granted ten days of privileged leave prior to my new posting, and I wasn't due to report to Nottingham until the end of April 1999. It was while I was on leave that something quite sad happened. It was 26th April 1999, and I remember watching the BBC One lunchtime news; the newsreader was Anna Ford, and she seemed anxious and clearly upset about something. I learned that earlier that morning one of her friends had been murdered.

Jill Dando was an English journalist, television presenter and newsreader. She spent most of her career at the BBC and was the corporation's "Personality of the Year" in 1997. At the time of her death, her television work included co-presenting the BBC One programme *Crimewatch*, with Nick Ross. On the morning of 26th April 1999, Jill Dando was shot dead outside her home in southwest London. It prompted the biggest murder inquiry ever conducted by the Metropolitan Police, and the country's largest criminal investigation since the hunt for the Yorkshire Ripper. A local man, Barry George, was convicted and imprisoned for the murder, but was later acquitted after an appeal and retrial. The case remains unsolved.

The CTT posting was going to be where I would eventually start wanting to learn about the subjects that most people do at school, such as English and maths. As a CTT instructor I was responsible for visiting some of the public schools in Nottinghamshire and Derbyshire. Each school had a CCF (Combined Cadet Force) detachment, and each detachment had a contingent of RAF, Army and Royal Navy cadets – these were young people in years ten, eleven, Key Stage 4 and Sixth Form, or Key Stage 5. Each school had its own officers, which were staff. During each day they would teach their respective lessons, such as maths and science, then once a week for half a day – normally one of the afternoons – they would parade with the young school students as CCF. The first year in the CTT I taught a combination of both military skills and adventure training.

During the half-terms, Easter and summer holidays, we would offer a course like the SCIC (Senior Cadet Instructor Course) for the cadets and AITC (Adult Initial Training Course) for the adult instructors. The adults would eventually attend a course at Frimley Park, which was about running a cadet detachment, learning about administration and safeguarding.

We would also offer adventure training packages, for both cadets and adults. Each military or adventure training course would normally last for one week, during which time AITC candidates had to learn drill phraseology, in order to teach a drill lesson – a method of teaching foot and rifle drill, both at the halt and marching. The candidate instructors would also have to teach a cadet GP rifle weapon lesson. This is quite an achievement, when you bear in mind that the cadets have the added pressure of GCSE or A-level examinations. Many of the adults too have jobs, and children of their own; they gave up their own time, once a week and at weekends, to help young people develop.

Hillary Clinton once said: "It takes a village to raise a child." This is an African proverb, which means that an entire community of people must interact with children, so that those children grow and develop in a safe and healthy environment; all the villagers look out for the children. In the U.K. and all around the world, a lot of children are lucky enough to go to school. Those children may also attend sports clubs and organizations such as the

Cubs, Brownies, Scouts and Cadets; the whole community is helping each other's kids to develop.

Not that the status of "Mum" doesn't carry with it a vast amount of responsibility; indeed, in some cultures around the world, Mum becomes a matriarch, the head of a family. When I was a child my friends and I all called each other's mums "Mum".

I made quite a few friends at Chilwell, both military and civilian. There was a Padre there that I knew from Angola; he had been attached to HQ 49 Brigade. Members of the Royal Army Chaplains Department give spiritual support, provide pastoral care, offer moral guidance and counselling, and they normally travel wherever a unit deploys to. I met him while I was attached to the Welsh Guards. I had only been in Chilwell for a day, when the Padre popped into various offices to say hello; he was well known in the station. He had a great interest in the schools our unit supported. While in Angola he had set up a school for orphaned children, who had been radicalized and made to take a cocktail of narcotics, then smuggle them and weapons into neighbouring countries, like Namibia to the south and Congo to the north.

One of the instructors in the CTT was Robert, a Sergeant from the Staffordshire Regiment; he was tasked with showing me the ropes and daily routine of the CTT, and visiting schools. During my first week, Robert and I invited the Padre to join us in Beeston and Nottingham; it was easy enough to walk into Beeston, have a drink then catch a bus into Nottingham. If anyone ever says that Army Padres are teetotal, they are lying! Our Padre liked to drink German beer. It is made from only the purest of ingredients and must conform to German Purity Law; an inspector can enter a brewery totally unannounced to check. This works to the advantage of a brewery, though, because the brewery then receives a seal of approval. The hops are organic and the water is pure spring. One thing

I found interesting is that, providing you drank some water, you wouldn't suffer a hangover the following day, because German beer has no chemical additives.

That evening, we bumped into "Dabber", the Detachment Warrant Officer of the University Officer Training Corps. Dabber had been the RSM of the First Battalion Worcestershire and Sherwood Foresters. It was Dabber's unit that I would be attached to for a week in Capel Curig, in North Wales, two weeks later.

So, now we knew each other it was time for a beer.

Later that evening, the Padre said to me: "So, Mark, what GCSEs do you have?"

"None?" I said.

The Padre replied: "No GCSEs? You'll have no A-levels, then?"

"Nope," I replied.

"Have you ever thought of doing any?"

"Not really, no," I said. I hadn't thought about any educational courses.

But I knew that I only had a few years left in the Army, and at some stage I would need to start the process of resettlement, ready for when I retired from the forces. I had no idea what I would do. It reminded me all over again of when I was at school, 21 years before. I supposed I could always drive or do security work.

The Padre advised, smiling: "You really should think about maths and English – and, if possible, a science course. There are lots available for adults – which is what you are now, Mark."

I didn't have any qualifications which would be of any use in civvy street; not much demand out there for weapons instructors or NBC instructors. I had plenty of adventure training qualifications, but that was it.

While out on the lash in Nottingham, we walked past a college, and the

Padre said: "That's where you need to go and find out about courses, Mark."

Over the next day or so I thought about what the Padre had said. I decided I would go and enquire.

Nottingham Community College had all sorts of interesting courses, and some of them didn't need any prerequisites. I was asked questions about what I taught in the forces, and they enrolled me onto a course there and then – and it was free! I would earn a qualification to assist in teaching literacy, to people who struggle with reading and writing. The whole course was eight weeks long; just two evening sessions each week.

The course was similar to and reminded me of the Basic Instructional Techniques (BIT) course available to forces personnel, in which I only needed to prepare one literacy lesson and another lesson of my choice. For my literacy lesson I chose simplification of text, and for the lesson of my choice I taught a three-star kayak session; my tutor observed from a RIB (rigid inflatable boat).

Eventually, the Padre sat me down and said: "We need to do G.C.S.E. maths and English, Mark. You can do this."

Chilwell had an Education Centre, where I was coached by the Padre. He gave me two books to read and DVDs to accompany them. One was a book called *Daz 4 Zoe* by Robert Swindell; I also read *Frankenstein* by Mary Shelley and watched the film. I was authorized to take my GCSE English exam at one of the schools I provided support for.

On the morning of the English exam I travelled to one of the Derby schools, in my combat kit. There were two other adults there, also taking the exam. We did the exam with everyone else in year eleven, in the school main hall; year eleven were all dressed in their school uniforms, though some would get changed into their combats at lunchtime, ready to attend CCF that afternoon.

For my maths I did night classes at Derby University. It wasn't GCSE, but an equivalent regulated level 2 maths course. That course lasted for the autumn term, during the fireman's strike of November 2002. There was a gentleman on the same maths course, who had a PhD in English Literature, but in order to teach English at a school or university, he needed a regulated level 2 maths course. He was a bit like me with maths: not very confident; he had been attempting maths unsuccessfully for two years.

I did my EPC (Education for Promotion Course), which all Sergeants needed to take, and the EPCA (Education for Promotion Course Advanced), for soldiers who are eventually promoted to WO (Warrant Officer), but they weren't regulated courses, so they were of no use for what I wanted to pursue.

I now firmly believe that GCSE exams are the most important in anyone's life. A-level courses might decide whether a student attends university, but it is the GCSEs which dictate the university a student will be enrolled at.

Over the remainder of that term and the first part of the spring term, I had helped the Padre out at key events in the British calendar, such as Remembrance Sunday, Lent and the run-up to Christmas. Then, just before spring half-term of 2003, I received my results for the maths course I had done. I already had my GCSE English results some weeks earlier; they had been brought to me along with the certificate, by the Detachment Commander of a CCF detachment of the school where I had taken my English exam. When he gave me the envelopes containing the results and certificate, he smiled and thanked me. I think he already knew my results, but I didn't want to open them until I saw the Padre.

I was running ranges at Beckingham near Newark, and the Padre had informed me that he was going to visit, so I made sure I had both envelopes with me. The day of the Padre's visit arrived and I went to have a brew with him, armed with my GCSE English results, still sealed in the envelope. I was quite nervous, but I opened the envelope and looked at the results. I must admit they weren't what I'd expected: there were uppercase letters, lowercase letters and several rows of text, with titles such as *"Speaking and Listening"*, *"Reading"*, *"Comprehension"* and *"English Language"*.

The Padre was getting impatient: "Give me the chuffing thing here!"

He read the results and revealed that I'd got a B. I asked if that was good. He said: "Yep, that'll do." Then, he added: "You're de-thicking, Mark! You can actually talk."

On the run-up to Easter, I continued to give the Padre a hand and attempted my final maths exam; the consolidated results would be available just before Easter. The results sheet was eventually handed to me by my tutor. The results were laid out in a similar way to how schools might do, with envelopes laid out on tables in the school hall, though the maths results were easier to understand; each topic covered in maths had either the word *"Pass"* or *"Deferred"* after each title. I returned to Chilwell and let the Padre know.

"Now what do I do?" I asked him.

He replied: "You load onto an access course, Marky."

"Yeah, my tutor mentioned that," I nodded.

"What school subjects did you like?" the Padre asked.

"Geography was good," I said.

"What about Philosophy and Ethics with Geography; surely you can combine the two?"

I asked: "What's Philosophy and Ethics?"

I can only imagine what the Padre was thinking; I expected his usual comment, "Stone the crows, Mark, are you really this daft?" And a second or two later it came.

Easter came and went, and I found myself studying Earth Studies, combined with Philosophy and Ethics. Earth Studies was physical geography, an understanding of maps, weather, succession of vegetation and natural disasters; I was doing Geography without all the political, population and agriculture. As for Philosophy and Ethics, all I knew was that it was a bit like Religious Studies – hmm, maybe that's why the Padre suggested this course.

My tutor asked me what I was going to apply my access course to, and said I still had no idea. But it suddenly hit me like a freight train: I was training to become a teacher. After all, I had been working with young people for over a year and a half, I had GCSE or equivalent and I was doing an access course. The teachers in every school that I went to visit were very inspirational, and I wanted to be just like them.

Some of the teachers in the staffroom at one of the schools sat me down and said: "Right then, Mark, which university are you going to go to, and which course will you choose?"

I was about to reply, when Scott, one of the P.E. teachers, said: "Think about a pilot course, Mark: not meaning flying, but the first course of its type that a university might run; they see what uptake they get, then if it is worth it they continue to enrol the following year, to run the course for a further three years and so on. If you identify a pilot course that floats your boat, you may find the first year free."

Scott was a PE teacher, but he also advised post-sixteen students about UCAS (Universities and Colleges Admissions Service), and he coached newly qualified teachers (NQTs) and staff at his school about continued professional development (CPD). Scott was very valuable, and knew what he was talking about.

He explained that there was one course which stuck out like a sore thumb, at the University of Wales, Bangor: it was entitled "Outdoor

Education", and would be a three-year course. It was almost as if this was destined, and that everything was laid out for me; I just needed to make things happen. I was invited to several evenings, learning about the application process for university. I was doing this with the post-sixteen students, and I found vast amounts of inspiration from some of the young people I worked with. There were NQTs, and even some of the cadets who wanted to go to Sandhurst as direct entries, going through the UCAS process. They were determined to make the world a better place, and they were going to make it happen.

It was Scott, Major Kirkbride, the Padre and three teachers from Merrill College who would coach me through the UCAS application process. Two senior cadets I had taught on SCIC even helped me with my personal statement. Everything was fitting into place.

My boss was Major Stewart Kirkbride, a real leader, and he was going through the resettlement part of his career – or, as he put it, "demobilization". Major Kirkbride was a very inspirational gentleman. He had been in the British elite SAS (Special Air Service) at Hereford, working his way through the ranks, then commissioned, but was now back with his original unit, the 9th-12th Lancers. They were an armoured cavalry tank unit (or, as Major Kirkbride would say, "donkey wallopers"). Sadly, Major Kirkbride only stayed with us for six more months before he retired. I didn't find our next boss very inspirational; he tended to keep himself to himself. I firmly believe that he was a manager rather than a leader, which may have made him more of a bureaucrat, by whom things are done by the book – which may be useful in the RMP (Royal Military Police). He held the rank of WO1, and had only eighteen months of service left before he would eventually move to and settle in Canada. He had hardly any military instructional qualifications, but he had done a Unit Expedition Leaders Course (UEL).

Eventually I received information, calling me forward to attend an interview at Bangor University. For this, I needed to take with me an achievement folder, or "brag file", containing course reports and original certification of relevant courses I had done in the past, such as BCU (British Canoe Union), MLTB (Mountain Leader Training Board), as it was called, and ski qualifications. But my most precious certificates were my GCSE English and L2 maths course certificates. The file was quite thick, but it was bound to be, because of my age and the courses I had done. All my file had to be copied, so that the university could keep a copy for their own use.

For my interview, I was going to wear casual smart clothing, but one of the teachers said: "Does an English or maths teacher wear casual clobber, Mark?"

No they don't, but they must dress smart when teaching. I decided to wear a suit with a regimental tie.

I was very familiar with North Wales and the Snowdonia National Park. It is a haven for all enthusiasts of adventure training and adventure sports, such as kayaking, climbing and mountain walking. My interview was in front of a panel of three people, including a gentleman called Iain Paterson, the Director of Plas–y–Brenin, the National Mountain Training Centre at Capel Curig. He had conducted my training course as an MIA (Mountain Instructor Training Award), and had been the Director while I was attending other courses at Plas–y–Brenin. I shook the hands of the panel, and the Director said, in his Scottish accent: "Good to see you again, Mark."

He already knew what was in my file, as did the rest of the panel. They asked questions about my plans postgraduate, to which I replied possibly working within a county council LEA, or in a school as a member of support staff, ensuring safety requirements were being met by organizations in terms of outdoor education; possibly, alternatively, as a teacher of Geography or PE I was using real terms and speaking a totally different language to what I was used to – but it worked; it turned out that my file and my UCAS application were successful, and that I already had a vast amount of prior accredited learning to load me onto the course.

The Army were not prepared to help with funding my course, even through a student loan, so I had to self-fund my whole course. However, I would only need to pay a percentage of the normal fees, due to the course being the first of its kind at that university. The Army did provide me with some support, though, by allowing me to be on secondment from Nottingham to North Wales – this was invaluable, meaning I could attend all my lectures and projects; university lectures were each Wednesday and Saturday.

The rest of my time would be spent working on other courses in the national park, and continuing with my normal duties. One project was to build a three-mile walkway, in the forest near Swallow Falls, for people with disabilities or who found walking difficult. There was soon wheelchair access all the way round, a café and benches for people to rest on, while regaining their strength. The walkway comprised all sorts of surface, such as bark chippings, logs to walk across, stone pathways and, of course, Welsh mud.

Personal development was an essential part of the course, meaning that I had to successfully reach the next level up, in two fields of adventure training. I chose MIA Assessment and BCU Assessor Status A, Three Star, to train and assess level three inland kayak coaches. I also held a D32-D33 assessor qualification, but I still wasn't a teacher. My Outdoor Education course required me to attend Parish Council meetings, District Council meetings and Young Farmers Club meetings; there was also a requirement to work with students on other courses. Between us all, we had to organize three adventure racing training events, and for these we were given permission to use the training camp at Capel Curig, at no cost.

We (and when I say "we", I mean all the students who were doing my course and people on events organization courses) took part in all sorts of projects to do with the outdoors. It was a way of working together with other people, practicing negotiation, communication and organizational skills. Henry Ford once said: "Coming together is a beginning. Keeping together is progress. Working together is success." This quote applies to everything our courses were trying to achieve, and it applies equally in all schools. For example, two maths teachers plus two English teachers, with a sprinkle of biology, physics and chemistry, then add a dash of Humanities and a sprinkle of Modern Foreign Languages, art and drama equals a successful student. Everyone works as a very finely tuned machine.

Our individual Adventure Race Training courses easily provided support for the local community, and created an interest and taster sessions for people who might not otherwise get the chance to take part in such activities or events. Each course we provided had a cost of eight pounds per day, to cover the cost of food.

On the Friday afternoon, our eight students would arrive and be shown to basic accommodation, then before evening meal they would attend a totally informal map and compass lesson, learning symbols and grid referencing. After the evening meal, the students were shown how to do basic repairs to a mountain bike: puncture and tyre removal, replacing a chain link and cleaning a mountain bike. Later on the Friday evening we would all walk to the Tan-y–Coed Hotel and Cobdens Hotel, both of which had nice bars.

Then, on the Saturday morning, after breakfast, the students had a lesson in First Aid and what to pack in a day pack, for a quality mountain day. We would then navigate our way to the top of Moel Siabod, stopping every so often to identify features on the ground and identify them on the map. Later on the Saturday, the students attempted a rope event, which was abseiling near Llanberis. After an evening meal, the students were shown a kayak and canoe, along with the equipment that a canoeist and kayaker would wear, such as a helmet, buoyancy aid, cagoule, spray deck and the various paddles.

On Sunday, all the students took part in a walkthrough, talk-through adventure race, starting with trekking from Capel Curig Training Camp. There were no mountains to climb, and most of the trekking was through forest. After six miles, they mounted mountain bikes and, at a pre-planned point, one of the instructors would be waiting to help students practice changing an inner tube and minor First Aid. At the end of the bike ride, students were introduced to canoeing and kayaking for the remainder of the day, before departure.

It was surprising that the students' comments included the possibility of organizing one for their children, which we did during the summer months. I was amazed by some of the parents, who had done an introduction course and were now BCU (British Canoe Union) Three Star awarded; some were even interested in BMC (British Mountaineering Council) courses. They were all beginning to know what they were talking about, which filled me with an element of pride for them. Eventually, some returned on future courses, to get logbook experience and become trainee instructors and leaders. Even the Academic Dean of the University of Wales (Bangor University) joined us on several expeditions and wild camps.

We had conducted courses at the Joint Services Mountain Training Centre, (JSMTC), Indefatigable (commonly known as "Indescribable", "Unpronounceable" or just "Indi") on the Isle of Anglesey. I would often get a bit cross with some candidates presenting themselves for assessment, and even more so with logbook entries; a lot of the time there weren't enough logbook entries or insufficient information, and when asked questions about their "quality mountain days", the candidates would not provide suitable information or answers, but may have just copied entries from other people, or even fabricated their entries. I can remember several WOs and officers on the JSMEL (Joint Services Mountain Expedition Leaders) course, who had no idea where they had walked; they only wanted the tick in the box and something to add to their CV. They would be deferred, because there were lots of people within regiments who were worth their weight in gold as mountain leaders, but were being prevented from attending such courses. As a result, I wrote to the National Mountain Training Centre, making them aware.

On one assessment, or JSMEL course that we ran, there was a soldier from the Royal Engineers whose logbook was amazing. Foggy had spent a lot of time with the AYTs (Army Youth Teams), and his logbook was a full D-ring binder thick, with photos and hundreds of entries. To be successful in Mountain Leader assessment, candidates needed entries in their logbooks which were in the British Isles; he almost had sufficient acceptable entries from the various national parks within the UK, but most were outside the British Isles; most of his entries were in the Himalayas, including some of the highest peaks in the world, with mountain experience in the Alps and the Rocky Mountains. He was therefore anxious to attend a JSMEL course. He was registered as a trainee with what was the MLTB, and he had all the qualities which might be expected of a Mountain Leader. The best he was going to get though was a deferral, both on the JSMEL and the civilian equivalent, the ML Assessment, but only until he had sufficient UK entries in his logbook. Alternatively, I could offer him another course.

I sat with him and discussed over a beer his two options. It was like putting words into his mouth, as I explained to Foggy what he really needed. I said: "You don't want to do this course, do you, Foggy? Because there is another course that I will ensure you attend, not as an ML but as an International Mountain Guide – just up your street, Foggy."

Foggy replied: "Er... well, I want the ML qualification."

I said: "Foggy, you should be aware of the superior course that I am about to offer you. We can send three soldiers from the British Army – you and two from the Army Physical Training Corps – on the International Federation of Mountain Guides Association's course (IFMGA). You want to do the course and be a Bergführer, a Guida, Guide de Montagne, don't ya, Foggy?"

Foggy smiled and said: "Yeah, I suppose now that you've said it like that it would be a good opportunity."

"Oh, yes. You will be able to operate worldwide, and be one of only three members of the British forces ever to do the course, Foggy."

I explained that he would be a mountain guide, a ski instructor, qualified in search, mountain rescue techniques and ski patrol, and become highly qualified in advanced medical techniques.

"It is now February. I have my phone here, Foggy. All I need to do is push this button and your CO, who I know very well, will answer. Then all I need to do is sign some paperwork: bish, bash, bosh and all done; you'll be on the course before Easter. Waddaya say?"

Foggy said: "Ooh, er, ooh, yes, please."

I immediately phoned Colonel Steve Barr, Foggy's CO. I stayed on the phone for ten minutes and got Foggy's course approved; I just needed the boss of Indi and several other high-ranking officers to approve.

This is where a Padre always comes in handy, because he found funding. Foggy was away on a flight to Bavaria the following Wednesday, to start his courses. He would have to do the whole course in stages, both in summer and winter conditions, but he was already an expert skier, so he would master the art of becoming a ski instructor with no problems.

Foggy was an example of someone who deserved such a course; he displayed valuable qualities: Foggy was firm, fair and friendly. He was a leader, not a manager, and a very experienced mountaineer.

Getting Foggy this course also meant that I could summon another soldier to take Foggy's place, so no course places were wasted. I approached the awesome boss of Indi.

"Hello, ma'am. You know how I think you're fantastic? Please can I get another candidate for JSMEL. Please, ma'am?"

She replied: "Oh, go on then if you must, Mark."

If we were to convert the course qualifications (in terms of adventure training) that we ran from military to the civilian equivalent, the UEL (Unit Expedition Leader) would be the equivalent of the Mountain Leader Training course; both courses lasted for one week. The JSMEL (Joint Services Mountain Expedition Leader) is also a one-week course, which is the same as the ML (Mountain Leader) Assessment course. Both JSMEL and ML assessments are examinations, and each candidate is assessed for the whole duration of the course. Holding the MIA (Mountain Instructor Award) course, along with a D32-D33 assessor's course, an individual could assess, through observation of performance, any trainee candidates on both the military and civilian frameworks, to become Mountain Leaders, as well as attending Single Pitch Supervisor Awards (climbing) and Rock Leader courses.

From time to time, my boss back in Nottingham would create barriers to prevent me from attending university, which was somewhat sad. It was also his only friend, the RSM, who would try to throw a spanner in the works, but he needed to pass an assessment, and I was the one who would eventually become his assessor. My boss would also attend an assessment course, but he would be disappointed with his deferral, which was due to his logbook only having a page and a half of entries.

Many people would argue that we should pass individuals in senior positions, especially if they are the boss, but it doesn't work like that; assessors need to feel comfortable that the candidates are capable of performing duties that are required of them. Some assessors might just write a good course report, pass the candidate and forget about, it in an attempt to have an easier life from their boss, but when is the bullying line crossed, and do bosses and people in senior positions realize that they are crossing that line? Students work hard to achieve success, and handing out a pass to a student can devalue a course. There is a term called "conflict of interest" which all assessors, teachers and people in management positions need to be aware of.

I was now an enemy of my boss, so he would place barriers to prevent me from performing my duties, by placing me on extra duties and refusing to authorize events which were actually in his favour. This would have a knock-on effect on other people, and eventually things would turn around to come back and bite him.

Eventually, the day of graduation was upon me, and the rest of the courses at Bangor; I now had a degree in Outdoor Education, which was valued by outdoor centres, local authorities and schools. This did not come as welcome news to my boss, but to Indi it was like striking gold, because I could take more responsibility from the boss, who had more than enough on her plate.

The RSM also had the responsibility of Resettlement Officer, and I needed to attend a one-week resettlement course. Soldiers go through a resettlement process, prior to leaving or retiring from the forces, and this eventually leads to training in trades which could be of use. Part of the resettlement process involved a one-week course, which was compulsory;

all soldiers leaving the Army must have attended this course.

I must admit that I had a bit of an issue about travelling from North Wales to North Luffenham, not far from Rutland Water, to attend the course; even though I had completed my Outdoor Education course, I still felt obliged to attend a lecture/meeting at Bangor on the Wednesday, and a Young Farmers meeting that I needed minutes for on the Thursday.

On the Sunday of my arrival at North Luffenham, I reported to the resettlement centre and was shown my accommodation. I went for a walk around and identified where the classrooms were. The WO and Sergeants' Mess was nice, and the bar was really quite nice. It was like a hotel; there were even waiters and waitresses who brought drinks to your table and waited on members. Drinks in the mess are usually very cheap and plentiful.

After breakfast the following morning I was assigned a tutor. He sat me down and explained my options. Being a Pioneer, he thought that a factory or warehouse might be suitable future employment for me, which is also what my boss thought. He mentioned other opportunities which might be good, but reiterated that I should seriously consider the factory or warehouse option; he even had an application form, ready for me to complete. I explained that I needed to wait until later that day before I committed myself. He explained that he would need to inform my boss if I didn't comply with his instructions, and that I was missing out on a fantastic opportunity. I didn't want to seem rude or disrespectful, but this person had no idea about me, or any of the other people assigned to him. The remainder of the morning was about identifying valued qualities and skills that employers are looking for. I must admit, I was a bit lost.

Then, during a mid-morning break, I had a phone call from… guess who… the Padre. I was so chuffed to hear him.

I said: "Am I glad you're on the other end of this phone, Your

Holiness."

He laughed and explained that resettlement centre staff only know your cap badge; they will be driven by that information regardless of who you are or what qualifications you have. Even a level five qualification, like a degree, will not necessarily sway them to point you in the right direction. The Padre asked what I had done so far, and I told him that I had learnt about qualities and skills, and that we all had to draft a letter of application, or a covering letter for a CV. These were things we had completed at university, as part of my courses study skills, and I had a covering letter and C.V. on a floppy disc, both fully up to date. The Padre advised me not to fill in any application forms, but to just go with the flow. So that is what I did, until lunchtime the following day.

After I had spoken to the Padre, we had a lesson about what to include in a letter of application, and it was at that point that I decided I needed to leave the course. I found a memo sheet and wrote two pages explaining why I was returning myself to my unit. An RTU (return to unit) would usually happen only on medical or compassionate grounds, or if there were issues with discipline; many soldiers would face disciplinary action for returning to their respective units. My case was different; I needed to attend meetings for my course. I only had one year left in the Army – and they weren't going to make me pregnant! I only had several weeks before graduation, and I wasn't going to be pushed into staying on the resettlement course by the RSM or my boss; it just wasn't going to happen. There were no safety issues, no one was hurt and I hadn't broken any rules; I was merely returning to Wales to attend meetings, in my own car.

I knew word of my disobedience would soon get back to my boss and the RSM, so I phoned my boss and explained my reasons. He was somewhat quiet on the phone, then he hung up. The Commanding Officer at Indi was much more supportive, and I felt valued, relieved and happy.

Her husband worked for the Department of Education, and she was aware of my future intentions. She did mention that I would eventually need to return to Nottingham, to hand in all my kit, prior to retiring from the forces.

It soon reached a stage in my life where I only had six months left in the Army. My boss at Indi (Captain A) mentioned that there was an opportunity for me to go on work experience, with an organization called Skill Force. They were a provision invited into schools, to teach an alternative curriculum to students who may be difficult to reach. The school that I would be invited to was in Bassetlaw, North Nottinghamshire. I jumped at the opportunity. Captain A had experience working within a CTT (Cadet Training Team) and an AYT (Army Youth Team). She knew many people in the world of education and was a qualified teacher herself, displaying all the attributes and qualities expected of a teacher. Her father had been a headteacher, and was now working as an HMI (Her Majesty's Inspector) for Ofsted (Office of Standards in Education). Captain A advised me that it would be a good idea to do some voluntary work while on my work experience.

The teachers and staff that I met at Tuxford School were just like all the other teachers I had met; I felt very comfortable and supported. While at Tuxford I was invited to observe some of Kerry's lessons. She provided alternate provisions. I was also privileged to teach some lessons, and whenever teachers were sick I volunteered to take their lessons as a cover supervisor; I was becoming part of a finely tuned team of people.

During that summer I had been at Proteus Training Camp, not far from Ollerton, and I wasn't going to see the Padre for a day or so, when he was due to visit adults and cadets on a weekend training camp for the CCF. Each day, the CCF cadets would board coaches at Proteus, and get taken to either Beckingham Ranges near Newark, or to where I would be: Rother Valley Watersports Centre. The cadets would take part in a round-robin of kayaking, windsurfing, water-skiing and cycling – they would then choose one of those activities to take part in at a later date.

What I did find interesting was what a group of young people in the school's sixth form said. We were talking about qualities a person might have, when one of the girls asked: "Who is it that identifies those qualities?" I listened to the answers given, then reflected later on what we had all been talking about. Anybody can boast about their qualities, but it may be up to peers or employers to identify them in an individual.

Those young people did worry about their futures, but they also worried about each other. I wondered if worry was perhaps a good thing – perhaps even a quality to go alongside caring. I wondered if people need to have a certain amount of stress in their lives. All soldiers witness high profile roles, like that of the CSM or RSM, being very stressful. If those roles and other appointments create stress, what qualities would an individual need to fulfil those roles? They might possess skills, but they need qualities to reinforce those skills. Sadly, some very valuable people have a stress level which may get out of control, leading to anxiety and feeling down in the dumps, and ultimately to loneliness and eventually depression. This made me wonder if my RSM and my other boss had a degree of depression; if they did, what could I have done to help? I didn't know if I felt selfish, but the more I thought about it, the more I started to doubt myself and the more helpless I felt. All leaders need to feel supported by team members, and I wondered if I was supporting him enough.

Young people suffer with stress in the same way everyone does, but often, for most, there is a safety net from which they can bounce back. Having bounced back, they then attack with more drive, diligence and determination, especially when it comes to exams. When they display courage, respect and focus, it is almost like their qualities have strengthened; they are now displaying all the core values of the British

Army.

Author's Notes

I have been very privileged to meet everyone I served with and came into contact with.

Many people reading this book will have identified individuals who display qualities and behaviour that are very valuable. Out of all the appointments and positions that service personnel hold, it is true to say that a unit Padre and the role of Sergeant Major share very similar qualities: they both have a sense of humour, they display compassion and most of the time they will listen. They will identify soldiers who may be struggling, and provide help and support for all service personnel, regardless of cap badge or position within a unit. Above all, the Padre and the Sergeant Major have a quality which sticks out like a sore thumb: they care.

There are many soldiers out there who suffer with mental illnesses, such as PTSD, depression, anxiety and anger; the list of conditions goes on and on. Many people I worked alongside clearly had what might have been some kind of mental illness. The world of a Sergeant Major can be lonely place to be, especially that of the RSM; he or she are in the middle of a tug of war, with the officers at one end of the rope and everyone else at the other. I remember one RSM, whom I had known when he was a Corporal; as RSM he became very isolated and lonely. This person was about to leave the forces and go into a world he had no idea about; it was like he had forgotten who he was. I hope and pray that he got the help he needed.

In an attempt to help with mental illness, a lot of people keep themselves busy and hide their problems, when all they really need to do is just talk to someone: a friend. And, dare I say it, perhaps they need a hug.

Glossary of Terms, Abbreviations and Jargon

LETTER	PHONETIC	PHRASE OR WORD	MEANING
A	ALPHA	Ablutions	Toilets, shower and washrooms.
		All-in	Meal made from a combination of leftover compo rations.
		AK (AK-47 rifle)	Avtomat Kalashnikov: a weapon system developed in the Soviet Union by Mikhail Kalashnikov. The rifle is easy to use, hard to malfunction but easy to fix.
		ARAB	Arrogant Regular Army Bastard.
		ATR	Army Training Regiment: the establishment where recruits go to complete part of their basic training. Prior to 1998, these establishments might have been known as "depots", and a corps or regiment would have had its HQ in a depot.
		AWOL	Absent Without Leave: leaving duties without permission.

B	BRAVO	Babies' heads	Individual tinned steak and kidney puddings, in the old compo rations.
		Badge ("The Badge")	RSM or SWO, often used by the Household Division.
		BAOR	British Army of the Rhine.
		Badmin	Describes a person with poor organizational skills.
		Beasting	The term used to explain a very hard PT lesson or personal training session, or drill session.
		Bean stealer	A pad (married soldier) who lives in married quarters but uses the cookhouse.
		Bergan	Modern backpack which replaced the Larry large pack.
		Black nasty	Issued roll of black duct tape without which the Army would fall apart. Higgs Boson.
		Bn.	Battalion.
		Bootneck ("Bootie")	A Royal Marines Commando.
		Brag rag(s)	Medal ribbons.
		Brat	A soldier in the Junior Army; Junior Leaders/Soldiers.
		Bratty wagon	A van which sells hotdogs, chips and drinks. An awesome sight when on training areas in Germany.

		Brew (Army)	A mug of tea or coffee; in the Royal Navy referred to as a "wet".
		BRIXMIS	British Military Mission in Eastern Europe.
		Buckshee	Spare item(s) of equipment.
		Bug out	A phrase used to inform troops to quickly withdraw to a save location.
		Bull	To polish or clean to a high standard.
		Bundeswier	German Army.
C	CHARLIE	Cas-evac	Casualty evacuation.
		Chalk	A group of troops in aircraft.
		Chin-strapped	Very tired.
		Civvy	Civilian; members of the public who do not serve in the forces.
		Civvies	A serviceman/woman's civilian clothing.
		Civvy Bill	Civilian police.
		Clacky	Chocolate.
		Clagg	Cloud and mist.
		Compo	Rations/food issued while on exercise or operations.
		Cookhouse	The restaurant where JNCOs and other ranks eat meals.
		Coy	Abbreviation for "company".

		Crab	RAF.
		CROW	"Can't Read or Write": a WW1 term referring to new recruits or inexperienced soldiers who were illiterate.
D	DELTA	Declaration	A verbal statement that you have no live rounds or empty cases in your possession. Given after NSPs, range days and exercises.
		Diffy	Gone missing; lost items.
		Diggers	KFS.
		Dipstick	A numpty or idiot.
		Dobie	Washing (uniform/clothing).
		Dossbag	Sleeping bag.
E	ECHO	Endex	End of exercise.
		EOD	Explosive ordnance disposal.
F	FOXTROT	Flash-to-bang time	The time it takes the blast wave of an explosive device from detonation to reach you. May also refer to the time it takes someone to register something in their mind. That person might be a bit slow.
		Full Screw	A serviceman or woman holding the rank of Corporal (abbreviated to Cpl.).

G	GOLF	Gat	A slang term for a small arms weapon like a rifle. Personal weapon.
		Gibbering	Freezing cold.
		Gizit	Free items; short for "Give us it".
		Gong	Medal.
		Gopping	Disgusting, mucky, dirty or tastes disgusting.
		GPMG	General purpose machine gun.
H	HOTEL	Hasbeen	A retired soldier: "has been", all one word.
I	INDIA	IED	Improvised explosive device.
		IGB	Inner German Border (Iron Curtain), 1945 – 1990.
		INLA	Irish National Liberation Army.
		IRA	Irish Republican Army.
J	JULIET	Jack	A selfish person.
		JL	Junior Leader.
		J/Ldr.	Junior Leader.
		Joining Instructions	A document with information including travel to and from, dates, timings and equipment/kit needed for a course.
		J/Sld	Junior Soldier

K	KILO	KFS	Knife, fork and spoon, diggers or eating irons.
L	LIMA	Lance Jack	Lance Corporal (abbreviated L/Cpl.).
		LMG	Light machine gun.
		LSW	Light support weapon.
M	MIKE	Matlot	A sailor in the Royal Navy.
		Maze	A prison in Northern Ireland, close to Lisburn, which held terrorist inmates.
		Megaton	Unit referring to the yield of a nuclear device, measured in tonnage of TNT.; 1 megaton equals 1,000,000 tonnes of TNT.
		MOD-90	Army identity card.
		Monkey	Military police.
N	NOVEMBER	NAAFI	Navy Army Air Force Institutes.
		NATO	North Atlantic Treaty Organization.
		Nato	Tea or coffee, normally with milk and sugar.
		NI	Northern Ireland.
		NIGS	New intake or soldier straight out of training.

		NSPs	Normal safety precautions to check that all weapons are safe and have no obstruction in the chamber. Usually done after all weapon handling.
O	OSCAR	O group	Detailed briefing.
		"On me"	A term meaning "come to me" or "follow me".
		Other ranks	Soldiers below the rank of L/Cpl.
		On the lash	Out for a few beers with friends.
P	PAPA	Padre	Army chaplain, Father.
		Pads	Married soldiers who usually had married quarters.
		Pad's brat	A married soldier's offspring.
		Pit	A soldier's bed.
		Pongo	Slang term for an Army soldier used by the RAF, Royal Navy and Royal Marines (wherever the Army goes, the pong goes).
		PONTI	Person of no tactical importance.
		POW	Prisoner of war.
		Putties	A length of material wrapped around the top of each boot. Protection against snakebites to the lower leg.

Q	QUEBEC		
R	ROMEO	RHQ	Regimental headquarters.
		RMA	Royal Military Academy, often referred to as Sandhurst.
		RSM	Regimental Sergeant Major.
		RV	Rendezvous: a temporary location which troops need to be familiar with.
S	SIERRA	Sandhurst	A place in Berkshire where officers complete their training.
		Sapper	Royal Engineer.
		Scoff (Army)	Food.
		Scran (Navy)	Food.
		SLR	Self-loading rifle.
		SMG	Sub-machine gun.
		Soldier	An individual (male and female) who is in the Army of a government, risking their life in the process. The word comes from the Latin word *solidus*, the name of the gold coin used to pay soldiers who fought in the Roman Army.
		SOXMIS	Soviet Military Mission in Western Europe.
		Sqn.	Squadron. A troop of soldiers is about 25 strong, and there are 4 or 5 troops in a squadron.

		STAB	Stupid Territorial Army Bastard.
		Stag	Sentry or guard duty.
		Stasi	East German Secret Police.
T	TANGO	TAB	Tactical advance to battle.
		Threaders	Feeling drained, angry and fed up.
		TNT (Trinitrotoluene)	A conventional high explosive.
U	UNIFORM	Ulster	The province of Ulster is the northern part of Ireland, referred to as Northern Ireland.
		Ulu	Remote areas. Out in the "ulu" means out in the woods.
		Urn	A large container/insulated vessel, usually containing a hot drink.
V	VICTOR		
W	WHISKEY	Wannabe	Someone with ambitions of wanting to be…
		Webbing	A set of pouches attached to a utility belt.
		WO	Warrant Officer: a senior rank which holds different roles or appointments. Usually the rank a Sergeant Major holds.

		Wolfgang	Hero of the Cold War / a blue Bratty Wagon.
X	X-RAY		
Y	YANKEE	Yield	In military terms, the power which can be delivered by something – for example, a nuclear device may have a low yield (not very powerful), but a high-yield device would be very powerful (kiloton or megaton). Has other meanings when used in financial markets.
Z	ZULU	Zulu Time	GMT.

Acknowledgements

The publisher would like to thank Russell Spencer, Matt Vidler, Laura-Jayne Humphrey, Lianne Bailey-Woodward, Leonard West and Susan Woodard for their hard work and efforts in bringing this book to publication.

About the Publisher

L.R. Price Publications is dedicated to publishing books by unknown authors.

We use a mixture of both traditional and modern publishing options, to bring our authors' words to the wider world.

We print, publish, distribute and market books in a variety of formats including paper and hardback, electronic books, digital audiobooks and online.

If you are an author interested in getting your book published, or a book retailer interested in selling our books, please contact us.

www.lrpricepublications.com

L.R. Price Publications Ltd,
27 Old Gloucester Street,
London, WC1N 3AX.
020 3051 9572
publishing@lrprice.com

Printed in Great Britain
by Amazon